Incredible
JOURNEY
in the Steps of Greatness

by
James R. Ray

To A Fellow Servant –

James R. Ray

Psalm 27:1

Published by
BIMI Publications International
P.O. Box 9215, Chattanooga, Tennessee 37412

Great Travelers & their Incredible Journeys

Adoniram Judson

Rueban Torrey

Lady Jane Grey

Hudson Taylor

John Newton

E.M. Bounds

Charles F. Weigle

John Wycliffe

Statue of
William Booth

F.B. Meyer

Robert Raikes

William Carey

Statue of
William Tyndale

Amy Carmichael

David Livingstone

Robert Livingstone

John & Betty Stam

John Bunyan

William Cowper

Dr. Lee Roberson

Dedication

With grateful hearts

we dedicate this book

to Dr. Lee Roberson

and Dr. J. R. Faulkner

English, Indiana...
Little Village that touched the World!

There was not much there. The beautiful country road leading to the little Indiana town gave no clue to greatness. The plain and humble homes along the way left an impression of timelessness–a place where time stood still.

The sign "English" was the marker that revealed to those coming that way that they were in a town indeed. Without the sign the traveler might have missed the beginning or ending of the village. There was a church–a service station–a few scattered homes–and then more road beyond.

The cry of a little baby, born on November 24, 1909, in the village probably did not generate any undue attention with the locals other than with a few relatives and friends of the family. However, the birth of that little boy, Lee Roberson, was perhaps the tiny village's finest moment. What happened on that day in November 1909 would touch untold thousands of people and through those thousands–MILLIONS.

The citizens of English could never have imagined that one of their own would influence multitudes and nations in the far corners of the earth. It is doubtful if the present day citizens know much about the story. Amazingly, God had passed through their midst with hardly a notice.

At age 14 Lee Roberson was led to Christ by a humble Sunday School teacher in Louisville, Kentucky, where the family had moved. That teacher was Mrs. Daisy Hawes.

During his many years of ministry, Lee Roberson served the Lord as an evangelist and then as pastor of churches in Germantown, Tennessee; Birmingham, Alabama, and Chattanooga, Tennessee. At Chattanooga he initiated a multitude of ministries to "catch men" for Christ. There was the radio broadcast, which became *Gospel Dynamite*. A church newspaper, *The Evangelist*, followed which reached a record circulation of 75,000.

By 1983 there were seventy chapels around the city and in the surrounding mountains proclaiming the Good News. When most churches in America had not even heard of church buses, the church under his ministry and that of M.J. Parker was bringing in hundreds of people to hear the Gospel. The soul-winning ministry of Lee Roberson extended around the world with hundreds of missionaries being supported by the church.

Other ministries included Camp Joy, where 20,000 young people professed faith in Jesus Christ. Union Gospel Mission, a ministry to the down-and-out, recorded over 30,000 salvation decisions. A major University, Tennessee Temple, was begun in 1946 and has trained thousands of Christian workers, missionaries and pastors whose ministries continue to shape the world.

During the years Lee Roberson continued his ministry of evangelism, in addition to the ministry based in Chattanooga, preaching in and touching thousands of cities in America. Over the years he authored and published over 40 books. During the forty years of ministry at Chattanooga alone, 63,000 people were converted and baptized.

The great man would quickly give credit to the team of godly associates surrounding him through the years, especially to J. R.

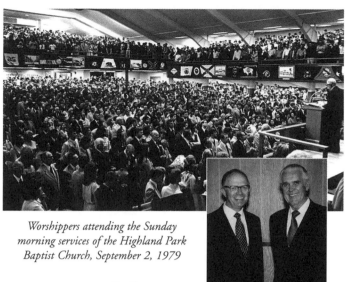

Worshippers attending the Sunday morning services of the Highland Park Baptist Church, September 2, 1979

J. R. Faulkner and Lee Roberson

Faulkner. J. R. Faulkner excelled in abilities that most men dream about. His spirit and zeal for this great work of God is almost unparalleled in this century. Thousands were motivated by his leadership to "be all that they could be." Under the leadership of these two men, Highland Park Baptist Church in Chattanooga, Tennessee, became one of the most visited churches in America.

A book about great men who have touched the world would seem inadequate without a word about these men who take their place with the spiritual giants of the ages. John R. Rice called Lee Roberson "the Spurgeon of our generation."

A prominent pastor, R. Gene Payne, surrendered to the ministry under Lee Roberson's powerful preaching. This author surrendered under the ministry of R. Gene Payne. How much we owe to him. How much we owe to Daisy Hawes, the Sunday School teacher who led him to Christ…and yes, how much we owe to English, Indiana …the little village that touched the world.

With grateful hearts we dedicate this book to Lee Roberson and J. R. Faulkner.

The Things
That Haven't Been Done Before
The ones who dared to do what we now take for granted

The things that haven't been done before,
Those are the things to try;
Columbus dreamed of an unknown shore
At the rim of the far flung sky,
And his heart was bold and his faith was strong
As he ventured in dangers new,
And he paid no heed to the jeering throng
Or the fears of the doubting crew.

The many will follow the beaten track
With guideposts on the way
They live and have lived for ages back
With a chart for every day.
Someone has told them it's safe to go
On the road he has traveled 0'er,
And all that they ever strive to know
Are the things that were known before.

A few strike out, without map or chart,
Where never a man has been,
From the beaten paths they draw apart
To see what no man has seen.
There are deeds they hunger alone to do;
Though battered and bruised and sore,
They blaze the path for the many,
who do nothing not done before.
Are you one of the timid souls that quail
At the jeers of a doubting crew,
Or dare you, whether you win or fail,
Strike out for a goal that's new?

-Edgar Guest

Foreword

With tender and loving hand,
Dr. James Ray touches the stories
of great Christians in days gone by.

As you read these accounts, you will
marvel at the amazing ways God uses
to get His message of salvation to
hungry hearts.

We commend Dr. Ray for his love for
the Gospel and for the stories of men
and women who have been used to proclaim the glorious news of salvation.

Dr. Lee Roberson
Pastor Emeritus,
Highland Park Baptist Church,
Chattanooga, Tennessee
Founder of Tennessee Temple University

Preface

The incredible journey recorded on the following pages of this book began over forty years past. The scene initiating this journey was that of a little wood-frame country church in the deep, green countryside of middle-Georgia.[1]

The church had stood since the turn of the century. Not much had changed in those years with the exception of the advent of cars, modern farm machinery and electricity.

The year was 1957 when a young minister accepted the invitation from the membership to become the pastor. Coming with inadequate salary and a small congregation, he set about to challenge the church to reach out to others. The little church was soon packed with newcomers. Excitement filled the air. Something was happening in the country. Through the faith of a young preacher in an out-of-the-way spot, God was pleased to reveal Himself.[2]

On a Sunday evening the author, then seventeen years old, stepped forth in response to a message to give himself away. Those fifteen steps to the old fashioned altar would lead to a path extending millions of miles. Those miles have brought the author into contact with the greatest lives ever lived. With a broken heart and tears, he made his way down a country church aisle to begin an...

Incredible Journey
In the Steps of Greatness!

[1] *Hardison Baptist Church, Byron, Georgia*
[2] *Reverend R. Gene Payne*

Contents

The Grey Family was of royal stock,
       an honor to be cherished,
but for Jane – it was a CURSE,
       ending her life at age sixteen.

Lady Jane Grey

1537-1554
The Nine Day Queen

A few miles north of Leicester in Leicestershire is Bradgate Park. Walking up the winding path leading to the Grey home, I passed beautiful historic trees. Those trees once witnessed the playfulness of two little girls. One was Jane Grey, who lived with her parents at the mansion situated at the end of the path. The other girl was Elizabeth, in later years Queen Elizabeth I of England.

Elizabeth would on occasion visit the Grey Family to play with Jane. The Grey Family was of royal stock, an honor to be cherished, but for Jane…it was a CURSE, ending her life at age sixteen.

Jane was an amazingly gifted and highly educated young woman. By the age of eleven, she was corresponding with leaders of the reformation in continental Europe. (Those letters still exist in Switzerland.) The tragic death of Jane Grey resulted from a power play for the throne of England.

Parliament had authorized King Henry VIII to nominate his successor to the throne. He had selected his two daughters Mary and Elizabeth to succeed him if his son Edward left no heirs. Should these three rule and die without heirs, a remote possibility, Henry directed that the throne would then pass to the family of his younger sister (another Mary).

This younger sister had died leaving two daughters, Jane Grey being the younger. Hence Jane Grey could become legal Queen only if Edward, Henry's son, and Mary and Elizabeth all died without heirs.

The Tower of London

During the early part of 1553, King Edward, then only fifteen years old, was dying. Upon his death, the next in line of succession was Mary, a passionate Catholic. The Duke of Northumberland, a devout Protestant, initiated a plan to bypass Mary, the legal heir to the throne, and in her place to install Jane as Queen. Part of Northumberland's plan included Jane marrying his son. This marriage took place with the complicity of her parents but against her own will.

As the plot unfolded, an attempt to capture Mary failed. Being forewarned, she fled to Norfolk, gaining time to appeal for help. Told of her succession, Lady Jane Grey protested. She had little desire to occupy the throne at the Tower of London. Her parents insisted. The circle of leaders surrounding Jane shamed her lest she not rise to save England by becoming Queen.

For nine days, Jane and her husband occupied the state apartment at the Tower. Meanwhile the scheme to replace Mary was parting at the seams. A force, led by Northumberland, to capture Mary at Norfolk had failed. The country at large knew very little of Jane Grey. Mary they knew as the legal successor to the throne. Jane was looked upon as a usurper. With all opposing forces in disarray, Mary entered London in early August with popular support.

Betrayed, Jane now found herself deserted by those who had forced her to become Queen. It was apparent that their chief motive had been their

Lady Jane Grey protested when she was told of her succession to the throne.

She had little desire to occupy the throne at the Tower of London.

Lady Jane Grey was no mere uneducated country girl. In a public debate at the Tower of London, she defended the Protestant faith with clarity so profound that her opponents were left speechless.

own political position. Her own father, seeing the unfolding of events, did an about face and proclaimed Mary as Queen. He returned to the Tower and found his bewildered daughter sitting on the throne in the council chamber. "Come down from there my child," he said, " that is no place for you." He then explained to her that she was no longer queen. She looked at him and in all the innocence of a sixteen-year-old girl asked, "Can I go home now?" The young girl was escorted from that chamber to another. Athough her new quarters were comfortable, she was now the prisoner of Mary.

Queen Mary realized that Jane had been used. She was fond of Jane and planned to release her. Being a close relative, Mary had known Jane all of her life. She secretly sent a message

to Jane saying that a pardon would be granted at an appropriate time. However, the political stage demanded another course.

Mary desired to re-establish Catholicism in England. Being surrounded by Papal advisors and facing strong Protestant revolt, she now found Jane Grey a serious liability. Jane could not now be set free without her becoming a figurehead for the opposition. There was a way out for Mary. If she could persuade Jane to renounce the Protestant faith and become a Catholic, this act would immediately disqualify Jane as a leader in the eyes of the Reformers.

Jane, however, would not deny her faith. Everyone around her, Protestant and Catholic, was guilty of religious politics. Jane had watched them use religious symbols to gain personal ends. Jane, however, caught up and used in their "web of deceit," was too pure to deny truth.

Queen Mary's next step was to involve Jane in a public debate in the Tower. Perhaps the Papal advisors could persuade her that she was wrong. *Foxe's Book of Martyrs* records this event. Lady Jane Grey was no mere uneducated country girl. She defended the Protestant faith with clarity so profound that her opponents were left speechless.

The debate ended with the young woman standing head and shoulders above her Roman debaters.

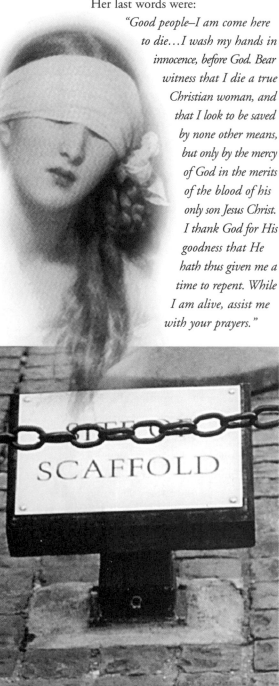

Queen Mary now saw Jane as a major threat to her throne. Jane Grey's innocence and her friendship with Mary in past days now all faded into nothing. **"Political correctness"** would rule. There was only one avenue left to Mary and that was to remove Jane Grey permanently from the stage...by DEATH.

On February 12, 1554, Lady Jane Grey went to the block in the Tower of London proclaiming the message of Christ. The night before she died, she sent her sister Katherine a copy of the Greek Testament urging her to read it. *"It shall teach you to live, and learn you to die. It shall win you more than you should have gained by the possession of woeful father's lands."*

From her window, Jane saw her young husband being led away to execution. From that same window later she saw his headless body being brought back in a cart.

She exclaimed, "Oh Guildford, the pain you have tasted, and I shall soon taste, is NOTHING to the feast you and I shall partake of this day in Paradise."

Then Jane herself was led out, a small sandy-haired girl dressed in a gown and a velvet cover on her head.

Her last words were:

"Good people—I am come here to die...I wash my hands in innocence, before God. Bear witness that I die a true Christian woman, and that I look to be saved by none other means, but only by the mercy of God in the merits of the blood of his only son Jesus Christ. I thank God for His goodness that He hath thus given me a time to repent. While I am alive, assist me with your prayers."

In the grounds of the Tower of London lies the block upon which she placed her head after a profound testimony for Jesus Christ.

Then she quoted a Psalm before handing her gloves and handkerchief to her maid. **The brutal executioner was shaken.** He was not prepared for this. He was used to victims cursing and resisting but this was a beautiful young Christian woman, gentle and innocent and only sixteen years old. She could have been his daughter. "Forgive me," he begged her. Jane replied, "You are forgiven. Do your work quickly."

She then tied the handkerchief over her eyes. Putting her hands out, she could not feel the block and cried out, "Where is it? What shall I do?" An onlooker helped her to find the block on which she laid her head, saying, *"Lord, into thy hands I commend my spirit."*

In Leicestershire, only ten minutes from where the author lived, there still stands the church where Jane Grey attended as a girl. Down the path leading from the church lies the ruins of the Grey Family home where Jane was born in 1537. In the grounds of the Tower of London lies the block upon which she placed her head after a profound testimony for Jesus Christ.

The church that Jane Grey attended as a child and young woman

Lady Jane Grey is mentioned in the *Guinness Book of Records* as the first sovereign queen of England.

Lady Jane Grey, if not the greatest, must surely take her place as one of the "purest" martyrs who ever lived and died for Jesus Christ.

The little village of Olney, tucked away in the heart of the English countryside, gives a visitor a sensation of timelessness.

OLNEY ⋈ HOME OF *Amazing Grace*

Almost 700 years ago the doors of Olney Church opened for the first time. For all of these centuries, the Olney church steeple has pointed up to heaven. Nearby, the River Ouse gently flows eternally on, while multitudes who have meditated in the reflections of the church steeple in its waters...have

John Newton
is most famous for his hymn "AMAZING GRACE," which is probably sung in every country of the world where Christ is known.

passed away. The author loves this little village that touched the world. One cannot come to Olney without sensing a past age, long gone, when God's grace was still amazing.

The little village of Olney, tucked away in the heart of the English countryside, gives a visitor a sensation of timelessness. Little has changed in Olney since the day the church doors first opened in 1325. Take away a few cars and one or two modern shop signs, make a slight adjustment in clothing, blink a couple of times and awake to a world of 300 years ago.

If you were standing in the town square, you would lift your eyes to catch a glimpse of the church spire rising 185 feet into the sky. If it

were on a Sunday morning, you would make your way down the street one block away to the lane leading to the church. Passing through the iron gates that day, you would have encountered a great crowd going in the same direction toward the massive wooden doors of the church. The church would have been packed with people who had come to hear the strangest preacher that Olney had ever known— a former slave trader, saved by the grace of God. That morning enroute to church you would have passed the old Vicarage where John Newton lived. On an attic wall in that Vicarage had been painted in black over the mantelpiece the following inscription:

"Since thou wast precious in my sight, thou hast been honourable." (Isa.43: 4) *"BUT THOU SHALT REMEMBER THAT THOU WAST A BONDMAN IN THE LAND OF EGYPT, AND THE LORD THY GOD REDEEMED THEE." Deut. 15:15* Those words have remained untouched since they were first put there by John Newton. Newton was pastor at Olney from 1764 to 1780. He had used this room, a large attic with two windows, as his study.

The mother of John was a Godly lady of non-conformist convictions. She was determined to bring up her son to know Christ. Her husband, John's father, however, was a sea captain who had been educated in Spain…and not devoutly religious. When the boy was only six years old, his mother died. Shortly afterward his father placed him in the care of servants and sailed away. About a year lapsed before his return.

Home of John and Mary Newton in Olney, England

The senior Newton remarried and John was placed in a boarding school. When John was eleven, his father took him on several voyages. For a few months he held a job with a merchant of Alicante in Spain. Following his father's footsteps, John turned towards the sea for his life's work. Eventually he was drafted into the Royal Navy. He was assigned to the ship *H.M.S. Harwich*.

When the captain of this ship learned that he was the son of a sea captain, he promoted him to quarterdeck as a midshipman. This opportunity was destroyed when John deserted ship. He was caught by military police and returned to the ship. After being placed in irons and then flogged with a cat'o-nine-tails, he was degraded from his rank. Off the Guinea coast John received his discharge from the navy. There he met a slave trader by

the name of Clow. Clow was reputed to have become wealthy through the slave trade. John persuaded Clow to hire him. Back home in England John had met a beautiful girl, Mary Catlett, whom he hoped to someday marry. Before this was possible, he would have to be able to support her. Now seemed to be his opportunity. Perhaps he too could become rich through slave trading.

In the country of the slavers John Newton now entered the darkest period of his life. Here slaves were captured and transported across the ocean to the plantations of the West Indies and America. Things went well for a short while with Clow. After some time, Clow began to mistrust John. He was left under the authority of Clow's African wife who treated him with uttermost cruelty. Here he became a "servant of slaves."

The native woman kept Newton under terrible conditions with no comfort. During this time he was given very little food and water. He became very ill but survived. At this time another trader established himself in the same area and asked if John could be released to work for him. Clow agreed and things improved. Soon Newton was trusted with a great deal of responsibility. His speech was appalling even to a slave trader, but his new owner felt he could be trusted.

When the ship *Greyhound* docked, a message was delivered to Newton. His father wanted him back in England. He at first hesitated. Here he could make a fortune with slaves and then have the means to marry beautiful Mary. The captain, wishing to receive the reward offered by Newton's father, put forward a lie. He informed him that he had received a large inheritance from a relative who had died in England. With that lying news, Newton became a passenger on the *Greyhound* and was bound again for home. On board ship with nothing to do, he occupied himself with drink. While he sat on the deck, verses his mother had taught him floated across his mind. To disarm these verses, he twisted them. The captain of the ship was appalled at Newton's oaths and asked him to refrain.

On one night of the journey Newton awoke to hear someone cry, "SHE'S SINKING." Rushing to the deck, he worked with the sailors to save the ship. After stuffing leaks with beeswax and dyer's wool, part of the cargo, he turned to the captain and said, "If this won't do, may the Lord have mercy on us." His own words shocked him. What had he said? All night long he labored with the crew to save a ship that seemed every second to be lost. Just hours earlier he had twisted the verses

In the country of the slavers, John Newton entered the darkest period of his life. Off the Guinea coast he met a slave trader who was reputed to have become wealthy through trading. Newton thought perhaps he too could become rich through slave trading.

of long ago–put into his heart by a Christian mother. Although he was only six when she died, her influence was living in him on the deck of a sinking ship.

Through the howling winds of a mighty storm–through the blackness of a stormy night–the sweet still voice of his mother's verses uttered long ago were germinating in his vile heart. After the miraculous deliverance of that night at sea, John Newton was through with blasphemy.

At one time Newton was captain of his own slave ship. He made three voyages for this purpose. He treated rebels in his crew with severity. Offenders were flogged and put in irons. In the actual ship's journal which Newton kept, there is recorded in detail his experiences as a slave trader. This journal was later published and reveals the horrible evil of this trade.

On February 12, 1750, John Newton and Mary Catlett became husband and wife. John had found a position as Tide Surveyor in Liverpool, England. Here he and Mary settled down for nine years. Newton's path now crossed with certain Baptists and Dissenters. The ministry of George Whitefield had also influenced him.

By his thirty-third birthday it had become apparent to John that God was calling him to preach. For six years he sought to find a Bishop who would be willing to ordain him. Eventually, the Bishop of Lincoln consented and offered him the Parish church at Olney. At age 39 Newton, with his beautiful wife, came to pastor in Olney. The church had to be enlarged to accommodate the crowds that came to hear the man who had enslaved men.

A member of Newton's church, poet William Cowper, worked with him in producing the famous "Olney Hymns." These included such hymns as "How Sweet the Name of Jesus Sounds," "Glorious Things of Thee Are Spoken," and "God Moves In a Mysterious Way." John Newton is most famous for his hymn "AMAZING GRACE," which is probably sung in every country of the world where Christ is known.

In the autumn of 1788 John Newton faced one of the darkest hours of his life. He discovered that Mary was dying with cancer. He had idolized Mary and at times had wondered if he loved her too much. She lingered for a long time and died in December of 1790. John felt that this was the end of his world. He had lived with Mary for 40 years and now he would live another 17 years without her. He had lost Mary for a time...but he had not

Through the howling winds of a mighty storm at sea–through the blackness of a stormy night–the sweet still voice of his mother's verses uttered long ago were germinating in his vile heart. Later John Newton wrote the words for "Amazing Grace."

Mary Ray and John and Mary Ramsey sing "Amazing Grace" at John Newton's Grave. The grave is located on the west side of the Olney Church.

lost God. There was still a work for John Newton to do.

He opened his Bible at the funeral service and read the followering:

"Although the fig tree shall not blossom, neither shall fruit be in the vines; the labour of the olive shall fail, and the fields shall yield no meat; the flock shall be cut off from the fold, and there shall be no herd in the stalls, yet I will rejoice in the Lord, I will joy in the God of my salvation." Hab. 3:17

Newton published a work entitled "Thoughts Upon The African Slave Trade" and worked with William Wiberforce and others to abolish slavery. In his last several years his memory failed. Sometimes he would have to be reminded, even in the pulpit, what his theme was. Some of his last words were:

"My memory is nearly gone; but I remember two things; that I am a great sinner, and that Christ is a great Saviour."

He was 82 when he died. John Newton and Mary are buried on the west side of the church in Olney. Styles in his book *Olney's Amazing Curate* gives this account of Newton's last sermon: "In 1806 he preached the last time but as he addressed the crowd, his mind wandered back to the days of his youth. To a friend he said, 'I am like a person waiting for the coach to arrive and looking out of the window for it.' " On December 21, 1807, at the age of 82 the coach arrived for him and the old redeemed slave trader turned his heart toward home

...to meet his beloved

Mary.

The Adventures of an UNSAVED MISSIONARY

RIDAY THE 13TH, 1737, Ben was awakened by mountain-high waves breaking over and against the sides of the ship. The clap of the waves resembled the sound of thunder or the roar of cannons. The old ship quivering and rolling in the churning, raging sea gave him the sensation of being in an earthquake. Ben sprang to his feet upon hearing the sound of panic coming from the men on the deck. They were in a hurricane on the Atlantic. The ship was out of control and would not obey the helm. The captain shouted orders, but through the howling winds, no one could hear.

Thoughts of Jonah must have filled the young missionary's mind, for like Jonah he was a reluctant missionary running from God. Seasick and sick of heart spiritually, Ben trembled at the thought of death, but whether he went down at sea or lived to face people at home in England with his failure, it would all be death. A few hours later the storm was over. Ben took his pen and in his diary wrote the following paragraph:

I went to America to convert the Indians, but oh! who shall convert me?…I have a fair summer religion. I can talk well; nay, and believe myself while no danger is near; but let death look me in the face, and my spirit is troubled. Nor can I say 'To die is gain.' I have a sin of fear that, when I've spun my last thread, I shall perish on the shore.

Fear of death was nothing new to Ben. Two years and four months before, Ben had felt the sensation of impending death. The year had been 1735 when Ben and his brother Charles boarded a ship destined

> **Thoughts of Jonah must have filled the young missionary's mind, for like Jonah he was a reluctant missionary running from God.**

for Georgia, that remote and wild colony of Great Britain. Georgia had been colonized only a few months, and Ben with his brother Charles, hearing of the need of missionaries there, surrendered to go. Ben's godly mother, when she heard of his intentions to go to Georgia as a missionary, responded, "If I had twenty sons, I would rejoice if they all

This preacher traveled more miles and influenced more lives than almost any other man in English history. He rode a horse more than 250,000 miles in his lifetime for the sake of the Gospel.

were to become missionaries, even if it meant I would never see them again."

Once on board the ship, Ben and Charles witnessed to the crew of Christ. Also on board ship was a group of German believers. When a fierce storm arose, Ben feared for his life, and some of the other English passengers actually screamed in terror. All the while the German believers remained calm and sang hymns right through the storm. Ben asked the Germans how they could be calm through such a trial, and they replied, "None of us are afraid to die." Ben noted that day in his diary the difference when true faith and a lack of faith face death.

Perhaps Ben would have been less fearful of death had his motives been purely the will of God and the conversion of the Indians. Like many missionaries who have followed in his path, Ben had the mistaken idea that crossing the ocean would make him, somehow, different from what he had been at home. In a letter dated October 10, 1735, Ben stated his reasons for going to the mission field.

*y chief reason is the hope of saving my own soul. I hope from the moment I leave English shore,...to know what it is to love my neighbor as myself. I cannot hope to attain the same degree of holiness **HERE** which I may **THERE**.*

The Atlantic voyage of three and a half months being ended, the ship sailed into the mouth of the Savannah River in mid-afternoon of February 5, 1736. At eight o'clock the next morning, Ben with his brother set foot on the mission field in the Colony of Georgia.

The two missionaries with several others mounted a hill and knelt down and thanked God for a safe journey. They then proceeded to the settlement of Savannah. The whole of the thirteen colonies could boast of little more than two million people and Savannah, settled only months before, had only forty houses and was surrounded by swamps and forests. The principal buildings in this settlement were a courthouse, which served also for a church, a log-built prison, a storehouse, and a public mill for grinding corn. All the houses were the same size.

The next day, Ben was approached by a Moravian believer who asked him, "My brother, I must ask you two questions. Have you the witness within yourself? Does the Spirit of God bear witness with your spirit that you are a child of God?" Ben was surprised. Who was this man questioning him, a missionary who had come to convert the heathen? He replied, "I know that He is the Savior of the world." The Moravian replied, "True, but do you KNOW that He has died to save **you**?" "I hope He has died to save me," answered Ben.

Pressing the issue, the Moravian asked, "Do you **KNOW** yourself?" Ben confirmed that he knew but later wrote in his diary that his words were vain. The fact was—he did not know for sure that he was saved.

In the days that followed, Ben and Charles settled into the life at Savannah. While a house was being built for them, they stayed with the Moravian believers and were amazed at their constant joy and cheerfulness. Ben saw something in the

Moravians that he wanted but knew in his heart he did not have.

They had been in Georgia for nine days when they made their first contact with the Indians. They were visited by Tomo-Chachi (the Indian chief whom Oglethorpe had taken to England some time before) and half-a-dozen other Indians. Tomo-Chachi, speaking through a woman interpreter, said, "I am glad you are come. When I was in England, I desired that some would speak it. I will go and speak to the wise men of our nation, and I hope they will hear."

The chief's wife, who had accompanied her husband, gave a jar of milk to the missionaries as emblematic of her wish that they might feed the Indians with milk, for they were children. She then gave them a jar of honey symbolizing their desires that the missionaries would be sweet to them. Ben was overwhelmed. Here at last were the heathen, yearning to hear the Word of God.

Ben's first letters back home from the field told of great opportunity and interest in the Gospel. With the arrival of spring and summer, Ben, now settled, began making contact with the Indians. He discovered some similarities between their primitive belief and his own. The Indians believed that God lived in the sky and had two others with Him—three in all. They were not sure if He was their creator, but they believed He had made men. When Ben offered the Indians a book that would tell them many things about the "Beloved One of the skies," they returned the disappointing answer that they were in war and would hear it later if a convenient time came. Ben now discovered that although the Indians had an interest in Christianity,

Near the spot where a church is now located on St. Simons Island, Georgia, Ben held open-air meetings in 1736 with George Whitefield.

their hearts were the same as those he left in England—hard and stony.

After some months, a disappointed young missionary sat down and wrote in his diary about the people he had come to

America to convert. No longer were they described as "Little children eager to learn and anxious to do the will of God." Ben's evaluation now was:

They have no religion, no laws, and no civil government. They are all, except perhaps the Choctaw, liars, gluttons, drunkards, thieves and dissemblers. They are implacable, unmerciful, murderers of fathers, murderers of their own children (it being a common thing for a son to shoot his father or mother because they are old and past labour, and for a woman to throw her child into the next river because she will go with her husband to war).

en was a failure with the Indians. He now began to make excuses. He was preaching to the English at Savannah, and one reason he gave for not reaching the Indians was that he could not find a replacement for his English work. Later, he went so far as to state *"that he could not find any Indians on the continent of America who had the least desire of being instructed."*

Abandoning his goal of reaching Indians for Christ, Ben now endeavored to build a great English work at Savannah. At first, all went well. He spared no sin, and crowds flocked to hear him preach. When the richer citizens of Savannah planned a dance, Ben held a prayer meeting and the dance floor was empty while the church was filled. The storm clouds, however, began to build. Some resented the strict message and rules of the young missionary.

He insisted on immersion for baptism and preached against social pride in dress. He was accused of aiming his sermons at

particular people in the congregation, and the fear of being pointed out and preached at began to have a marked effect on the attendance. Others accused him of playing

I went to America to convert the Indians; but, O! who shall convert me?...

favorites. On one occasion, a woman whom Ben had offended knocked him down and cut off a handful of his hair. Then he was criticized for being shoddy in the pulpit.

A key point of trouble came when Ben refused to propose marriage to the daughter of a prominent family in the colony. He had actually wanted marriage with Sophy, but permission was refused by the local mission authorities, and Sophy ran away and married another admirer. Ben was thirty-four at the time, and his disappointment was painful. Later, when Ben had to exercise church discipline against Sophy, he was accused of using the church to vindicate his wrath against her.

At last, charges were brought against him, and although Ben had many friends at Savannah, the strain had been too much. He realized that his effectiveness was past as a preacher to the English in Savannah. Had he stayed and fought, he might have won his battle, but the damage to his ministry by this time was irreparable. The magistrates gave orders that Ben could not leave the colony until the case was settled.

That same evening, Ben, with four other fugitives who had reasons for wishing to leave the colony, started in an open boat for Port Royal, in South Carolina. It took much hard rowing against the waves on the journey up the coast, but on December 6, 1737, they reached their destination, from which they sailed to England.

On his way back home from America in 1738, Ben took up his pen and summarized his state of heart and mind:

"I went to America to convert the Indians; but, O! who shall convert me?...It is now two years and almost four months since I left my native country in order to teach the Georgian Indians the nature of Christianity, but what have I learned myself in the meantime? Why, what I the least of all suspected; that I WHO WENT TO AMERICA TO CONVERT OTHERS WAS NEVER MYSELF CONVERTED TO GOD."

A few months later, Ben found true faith in Christ and assurance of real salvation. The results of this experience led Ben into a ministry that saved England from a French-type revolution. He became one of the greatest Christian workers in British history. He preached more sermons, traveled more miles, published more books, wrote more letters, built more churches, waged more controversies and influenced more lives than almost any other man in English history, riding a horse more that 250,000 miles in his lifetime for the sake of the Gospel.

It was on March 2, 1791, that an eighty-eight-year-old man of God lay down to die in his home in London. Looking out his window, he could see across the road BunHill Cemetery, in which rested the bodies of **John Bunyan, Thomas Goodwin, Susanna Wesley, John Owens** and many of the greatest saints who ever lived. In just hours, Ben would be in their number. Perhaps the old man thought, *"What if I had quit after Georgia, never again to preach? How much I would have missed!"*

Ben had lived many lives in one and with such fervency that Southey was led to comment: "I consider him as the most influential mind of the last century."

At one time, he had been an unsaved missionary, then as a true believer the most abused evangelist and separatist of this country. Every church door in England was locked in his face. God used him to touch the lives of millions. **Today in England's grandest cathedral, Westminster Abbey, there stands a marble monument dedicated to this missionary to nations, to BEN...that is...**

JOHN

BENJAMIN

WESLEY.

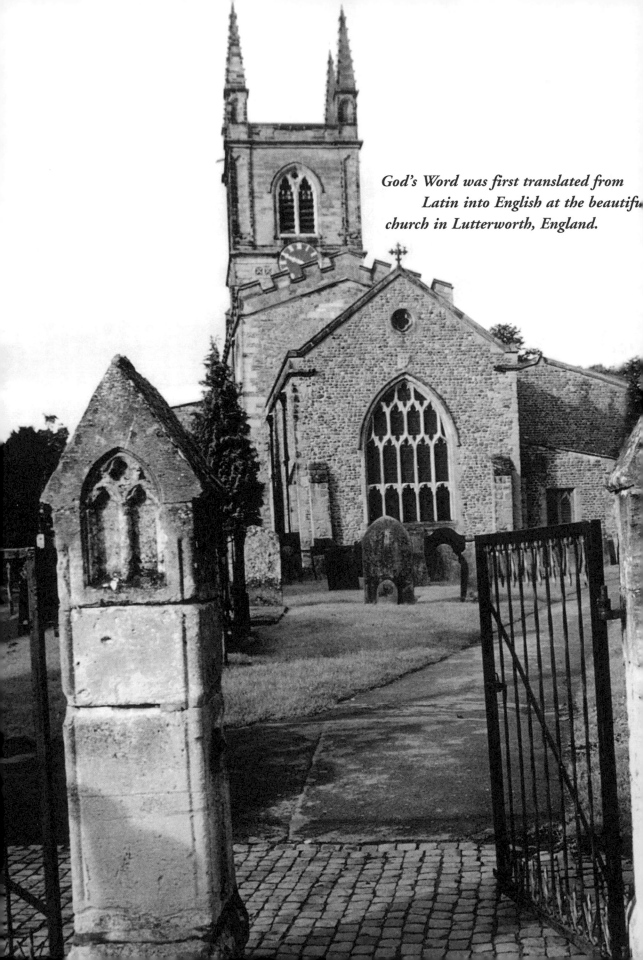

God's Word was first translated from Latin into English at the beautiful church in Lutterworth, England.

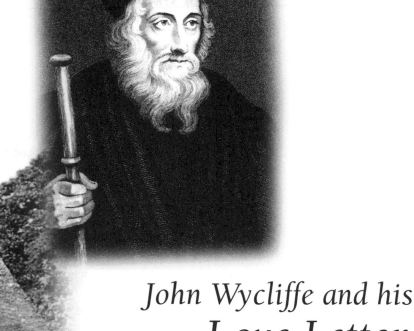

John Wycliffe and his
Love Letter from Lutterworth

Away up in Yorkshire is a tiny village by the name of WYCLIFFE. This is the only place in all of England called by that name. Born in this village in 1324 was a person who would literally change the world.

They called him John, John of Wycliffe, then John from Wycliffe and later simply John Wycliffe. Mary and I wanted to trace the roots of this famous Christian who impacted all of Christendom. Locating the tiny village on a map, we made our way to Northern England to Yorkshire.

Leaving the motorway, we drove deep into the countryside of beautiful Yorkshire. The country seemed forsaken except for fields and fields of green pastures feeding hundreds of grazing sheep. Eventually we found ourselves navigating one-lane roads closed in by thick hedges. At last we came to a wooden sign with the treasured words "Wycliffe–Two Miles." As we arrived at Wycliffe, the road ended at the edge of a roaring river. Wycliffe was located literally at *the end of the road.*

The village consisted of two or three houses and a church, all crumbling with age. The place seemed utterly forsaken. This church was the place of John's Catholic baptism in 1324. The priest who held the tiny baby in arms would have trembled had he known this child would someday shake the foundation of the Catholic Church.

Here by the river, this village at the end of the road, a man was born who would die in 1384 in another small English village called LUTTERWORTH. Lutterworth, although now bordered by the M-1, still retains much of its ancient antiquity. With the exception of the automobile and a small number of modern houses, the actual village has changed very little from the days of Wycliffe in the 14th century.

The parish church, once pastored by Wycliffe, situated on the highest spot in the town, was easily located. Beautiful ancient tutor houses and several shops adorned the narrow street approaching the church. Before exploring the church, I decided to stop at a tearoom located just down the path leading to the church.

The small restaurant had a very simple arrangement containing about six laminated tables. The tables were surrounded by local patrons and the echo of English chatter filled the room. Entering the teashop, I spotted an empty table near the window and made my way to a chair. The chatter ceased immediately as I entered the room and I could feel the penetrating gazes of all the locals. I had hoped not to be noticed but my three cameras gave it all away. A *foreigner* had entered the teashop.

I could feel the silence of death. The locals were sizing me up. As I placed my cameras on the table, I felt like a "super tourist." I could sense the searching gaze of the locals. Looking up–sure enough–eyeballs were stretched to their limit at this obvious stranger.

The space was about a ten to fifteen foot square room with a glass showcase containing several cakes. Fastened to the wall was a simple sign with the words "ONLY FOOD PURCHASED IN THIS RESTAURANT CAN BE CONSUMED HERE." Behind the counter three ladies dressed in white outfits stood in a row staring. I wasn't sure whether I should approach the counter with an order or wait it out for one of them to come to the table. I was not even sure they would come.

Whatever happened, I did not want to speak loudly with my American accent. Already the English chatter of the locals had ceased. Now they all waited with intense interest for me to make an order. This would help them further analyze this intrusion into their small village. From across the room, one of the women called out, "What would you like, dear?" I had seen a sign chalked on a menu board out front upon entering that read: "FRESH MEAT PIES, FRUIT PIES WITH CUSTARD."

I answered in my southern American accent, "I'll have apple pie and custard." "Thank you, dear," she replied as she disappeared into the small kitchen behind her. A few moments passed and she approached my table, leaned over and asked, "Now what did you say you wanted?" I repeated my order only to learn that they had no apple pie. I opted for cake with fresh cream.

She disappeared again into the small kitchen filled with pots and pans almost up to the ceiling. By this time the locals were really staring. Out from the kitchen came the lady in white, followed by two others with a large flat book. Laying it on my table in front of me, she asked if I would sign the register.

The little restaurant came to life. The chatter started up again. It was almost as if I had been accepted. They knew who I was. A "very English" lady explained to me that the people in Lutterworth were very friendly. She was from London herself but had lived in Lutterworth for many years.

A gentleman nearby told me of his trip to America and Disney World in Florida. The three ladies in white were only too happy to abandon their restaurant and customers for a special picture outside under their tearoom sign. Leaving the little tearoom, I pondered the scene. Perhaps these locals were descendants of people who centuries ago had known and followed John Wycliffe. The possibility existed.

John Wycliffe was born at a time when the darkness of Catholicism ruled almost all of Europe. Here and there across Europe a light of Gospel truth would flash as a star through the dark night sky. No sooner would its gleam be noticed than it would be snuffed out by a pagan system, like a falling star seen only but for a moment. The man born at the "end of the road" in an obscure village in Yorkshire would break the spell of darkness–forever.

The common population of the country at the time was composed of peasants. Faithfully they attended the Catholic churches only to hear words in Latin that could not be understood. The people would enter the churches, stand or kneel for hours and leave with their souls still in spiritual darkness. The church held the people in bondage through its sacraments and a fear of judgment. Without the light of Scripture, the people's only hope lay in payment to the corrupt priests and masses for the dead.

It is important to note that there were no reforming movements in England in

> *The common population of the country at the time was composed of peasants. Faithfully they attended the Catholic churches only to hear words in Latin that could not be understood.*

The parish church, once pastored by Wycliffe, situated on the highest spot in the town, was easily located. Beautiful ancient tutor houses and several shops adorned the narrow street approaching the church.

Wycliffe's day. The Catholic Church was the only church the people knew. In their minds there was no other. When John Wycliffe stood against the doctrines of the church, he was standing alone. His was a lone and single voice in a sea of paganism.

Wycliffe had a special enmity for the traveling Friars. The Friars would travel about the country preaching their superstitions and offering pardons for sins with proper payment. In 1360 Wycliffe published his "Objections to the Friars," exposing their notorious corruption. The Friars were enraged.

Wycliffe wrote concerning the begging friars, "He stuffs the people…with garbage." The writings and preaching of Wycliffe were powerful elements.

At the time Parliament was engaged in a struggle with the Pope at Rome. The issue involved the sovereignty of the country. England was drawing away from Rome. With the mood of the country antagonistic toward the Pope, Wycliffe now referred to him as "Anti-Christ, the proud, wordly priest of Rome and the most cursed of clippers and purse-kerver."

Under pressure to pay tribute to the Pope, Parliament sought counsel from Wycliffe. Parliament desired to keep the country resources from being carried away to Rome but feared a sin of disobedience. Wycliffe replied, "Who gave the Pope this power?" It was certain that this assumed authority did not come from God.

1n 1374 Wycliffe became the rector (pastor) at Lutterworth. Here, far away from London and Oxford, he could now complete his writings, including the translation of the Bible into English. At Lutterworth he pastored a local church filled with people who sought the words of God. The majority of Wycliffe's sermons that are still in print today were preached from the pulpit at Lutterworth. In 1382 the English Bible was complete. His papal enemies were incensed. One of them wrote:

"Wycliffe by thus translating the Bible made it the property of the masses and common to all and even women who were able to read. The gospel is thrown before swine and trodden underfoot, and that which used to be so dear to both clergy and laity has become a joke....This precious gem of the clergy has become...common to the laity."

Wycliffe responded: *"Christ and the Apostles taught the people in the language best known to them. Therefore, the doctrine should not only be in Latin but in the common tongue. If it is heresy to read the Bible, then the Holy Ghost himself is condemned who gave in tongues to the Apostles of Christ to speak the Word of God in all languages that were ordained of God under heaven."*

The Catholic Church in the 1300s was selling pardons from sins for money. Wycliffe took exception to this policy asking, "Who gave the Pope this power?"

There had gathered around John Wycliffe many young men. These young men had attached themselves to his ministry and now were sent throughout the land. Their numbers increased into the hundreds. Everywhere they went they "preached the Word."

Wycliffe's Bible men or "Lollards" impacted the country against the false doctrine of transubstantiation. They taught fervently the priesthood of the individual believer. The Pope summoned Wycliffe to Rome to answer for his actions. Wycliffe, who had suffered a stroke, replied, "Christ has needed me to the contrary, and taught me more obedience to God than to man."

On the last Sunday of 1384 during a service at Lutterworth, John Wycliffe suffered a third stroke. Faithful men took him in a chair out of a side door to the church rectory. Two days later, December 31, he died in bed.

Entering the gates of the church grounds, I felt I was walking on holy ground. So much had happened on this piece of property. Almost forty years after Wycliffe died, Catholic fanatics, appointed by the Pope, dug up his bones from the cemetery at Lutterworth. They then burned them and cast the ashes into the River Swift that flowed through the town.

Even that act by his enemies symbolized the life of John Wycliffe. His ashes were thrown into the River Swift there at Lutterworth. The river carried them into larger rivers, then into the English Channel, and from there to the oceans of the world touching every land.

Looking downhill from the church grounds, I gazed on the smooth waters of the flowing river. Entering the church, I saw the pulpit that he faithfully preached behind in 1374. There were the pews where common folk heard the Word of God in their own tongue. There was the chair used in 1384 to carry him out of the church after his stroke, then the door, the same door, out of which they carried him from the church for the last time. The long journey from the remote village of Wycliffe to Lutterworth had ended, but the world would never be the same. The world now had a Bible, a Love Letter from God, in a language they could understand.

Strolling through the ancient cemetery surrounding the church, I was awed by the messages inscribed on the graves. I spent the morning there...enjoying the faith of Christians long gone.

Almost forty years after Wycliffe died, Catholic fanatics, appointed by the Pope, dug up his bones from the cemetery at Lutterworth. They then burned them and cast the ashes into the River Swift that flowed through the town.

The faith of the people at Lutterworth was a direct result of John Wycliffe's "Love Letter from God."

Inscriptions from Graves at Lutterworth

"UNTIL THE SHADOWS FLEE AWAY"

"CALLED HOME"

"PEACE, PERFECT PEACE"

"HIS END WAS PEACE"

"AT EVENING IT SHALL BE LIGHT"

"I KNOW THAT MY REDEEMER LIVETH"

"I SHALL BE SATISFIED WHEN I AWAKE IN THY LIKENESS"

And this one:

"FRIEND IS THE QUESTION ON THY HEART ENGRAVED, WHAT MUST I DO TO BE FOREVER SAVED? IN JESUS IS THE SOLE REPLY, BELIEVE IN HIM AND NEVER DIE."

These graves told a story. These graves reflected a ministry that offered assurance. Where did the people of Lutterworth past gain such serenity, such assurance, such hope? They got it from their fathers and their fathers…from their fathers and…their fathers back through the centuries from the Bible, God's Love Letter, given to them by their pastor, **John Wycliffe**.

Here among these graves surrounding the church of John Wycliffe, I found hope and assurance from "GOD'S LOVE LETTER" –THE BIBLE. The people's faith represented by those graves at Lutterworth was a direct result of John Wycliffe's "Love Letter from God."

Multitudes today reject the message of Christ. The simple village folks–long buried in the little village of Lutterworth –will at the Judgment rise up and condemn Christ Rejecters. Why would missionaries go to the end of the earth to people who have no hope? They have in their possession a Love Letter from God.

The world waits to hear this message…a message that can save, forgive, and give **Hope in despair…**a message that can shine **Light into Darkness** and bring **Comfort in Sorrow.** This message of Jesus is found in this book–this love letter from God.

Dear Reader–what will you do with this message? Soon life will be over, our opportunities ended and like the people of Lutterworth, we will be in the grave– We must act NOW!–We must give ourselves to God NOW. The world still waits for this message from God. Pray…

"LORD - WHAT WOULD THOU HAVE ME TO DO?"

*Amy Carmichael left her life in Ireland to serve
the lost and the poor in India.*

Amy Carmichael's

Ireland

Somehow the old mills at Belfast made her live again. The author had heard of her, read of her, but the old mills were her footprints leading to greatness.

On December 16, 1867, Catherine Carmichael looked down into the face of her first child. Amy was the first of seven children to be born to Catherine and David Carmichael. How could they know that this little girl with deep, dark brown eyes would touch a world far away from County Down, Northern Ireland. In fact, Amy would touch the world at large with her writings which would continue to be published long after her death.

David and Catherine were devout Christians. They were determined to instill the faith of Christ into their children. Perhaps it was a motivation from God that led David to teach survival skills to Amy. She was taught to swim, to ride a wild pony and

Does it not make us long to leave our luxury, our exceeding abundant light, and go to them that sit in darkness.

to stick to a task until it was completed. Amy's parents sent the children down to the village with soup and food for the sick and aged. In a day when there was no state social scheme, this was greatly appreciated. Amy learned firsthand from her parents the grace of giving one's self away.

On occasions the brother of their pastor, who was a missionary to India, would visit the Carmichaels while on furlough. Often the missionaries would visit the family on Sunday afternoon. Amy listened intently as he and his wife told stories of India. Perhaps even there on those Sunday afternoons in County Down, God was planting a seed in Amy's young heart.

A few years later when Amy was in a boarding school at Harrogate, she attended a crusade organized by the Children's Special Mission. When the invitation was given, Amy realized that she, herself, needed to make a decision. At that moment, she invited Christ to take over her life and become her Saviour. This decision set the stage for her life's ministry.

The Mills at Belfast, Ireland

At age fifty-four, her father contracted pneumonia and died. He, who had taught her about God and shown her how to live, was now gone. Perhaps the motivation of his life now prompted Amy to "give herself away" as her father had so diligently done. She poured herself into working with children and caring for those in need.

It was early in 1888 that Mrs. Carmichael called the children into the dining room for a special announcement. All of the family money had been lost in a financial crisis.

They knelt together around a table and prayed. The family would trust God. He would provide as He always had. Amy had no doubt but that God would meet every need. Her loving father was gone but her loving eternal Father would never leave.

Step by step God was leading Amy into His will. She felt a special calling to minister to the working women of Ireland. The giant mills in Belfast used hundreds of poor young women in the work. Daily the young girls made their way to the mills to work long hours for the purpose of scrapping out a living. These poor mill girls were labeled as "Shawlies" by those with means because they were too poor to buy hats and covered their heads with shawls.

Amy visited the slums to invite these young women to the Rosemary Street Presbyterian Church. Two contrasting pictures emerged. On the one hand there was Amy with her burning desire to see these young women brought to Christ. On the other hand were the dignified Presbyterians whispering and horrified at the presence of such common stock in their midst.

The work with the "Shawlies" was growing. The stuffy Presbyterian Church was becoming packed with the poor ragged and destitute girls from the mill. Sometimes two or three of them would pray at the same time, this upsetting the faithful. The prayers of "the faithful" were answered when the crowds grew so large that a special hall seating five hundred was needed to accommodate them.

An ad appeared in a magazine advertising a building made of iron, which could be purchased for five hundred pounds. The family fortune was gone. It would take God to supply a sum like this. A few days later Amy, with her mother, visited an old lady for a cup of tea. It was a beautiful but monotonous occasion. The conversation of the "boring" visit included the need of a special hall for the poor mill girls.

The old lady mentioned this need to a friend who in turn asked Amy to lunch. Only a few days later Amy received a letter from the friend offering to purchase the hall. A mill owner donated land for the building.

Amy named the building "The Welcome Hall." Printed invitations were sent out

The Welcome Hall

inviting people to the dedication held January 2, 1889. A banner was placed above the platform reading "That in all things He may have the pre-eminence."

The invitation read:

> *"Come one, Come all,*
> *To the Welcome Hall,*
> *And come in your*
> *Working clothes."*

Two students of American evangelist D.L. Moody led in the opening services with a series of meetings. Each night as the invitation was given, people came to Christ. It was at this meeting that the gospel song "I know Whom I Have Believed" was sung for the first time in the British Isles.

Hudson Taylor came to Belfast to take part in meetings sponsored by Keswick. His words were stirring to Amy's young heart. Taylor said,

"Every hour four thousand pass through the gates of death into the darkness beyond—Saviorless, hopeless."

Amy later wrote: *"Does it not stir our hearts to go forth and help them? Does it not make us long to leave our luxury, our exceeding abundant light, and go to them that sit in darkness."*

She did go—to Japan—to China—to Ceylon and finally to INDIA where she spent the remaining fifty-three years of her life for Christ. She authored thirty-five books. Her writings were published in fifteen languages and twelve of them in Braille. The influence of Amy Carmichael's life continues through her writings and second generation converts. The Welcome Hall continues to preach the Gospel in Belfast—after one hundred years.

On January 1, 1951, Amy Carmichael closed her eyes in India for the last time. The long journey of a young girl in County Down to the grave in India was over. The last steps had been taken but it had been an...

Incredible journey with God.

How A
Man-eating Shark Filled Up A Church!

Charles F. Weigle was a legend.

The famous author of "No One Ever Cared for Me Like Jesus" on occasions led singing for Billy Sunday. He related to me of hearing D.L. Moody. Once he met William Jennings Bryan on a train.

As a young student, my wife Mary was assigned at Bible College to keep his room ready. Tennessee Temple University had built a special apartment for him at the school. The president of the school at the time, Dr. Lee Roberson, felt that the presence of such a man on campus would be a positive influence on the students.

Mary often would hear the great man writing songs, singing and playing the piano. He would call her into the music room and sing his new songs to her. One of our treasured possessions is a letter written to us on the occasion of our wedding when the great man was 92 years old.

When Charles Weigle came to our church for special meetings, I listened intently to the stories and events of an era long gone. There was the citywide meeting in an Ohio city. Billy Sunday and other friends urged Charles to abandon the plans for the meeting. "That town is a preacher's graveyard," they told him. Still determined that God was in it, Charles Weigle proceeded. He remembered, "We build a huge tin tabernacle. I preached my heart out for two weeks. Then I gave an invitation and 2000 people responded receiving Christ."

Most unforgettable was the account of the shark that filled a church. "I was preaching a meeting in California. On Monday night the meeting was almost bare with few people attending. That night in my room I knelt and prayed about the matter. I reminded the Lord that empty pews could not repent and believe. I asked God to fill the church.

Had I known how God would answer that prayer, I would not have prayed it. The next morning a member of the church who owned a house on the seashore invited me to come and swim from his private beach.

There I was out in the ocean enjoying the waves when suddenly something beneath the water brushed against my legs. Without thinking I reacted and grabbed the object. Immediately I realized that it was ALIVE –in fact it was a man-eating shark. I was afraid to let go. The big fish seemed angry. When it pulled one way, I pulled it the other from left to right. We were making quite a big splash. Panic stricken, I began working toward shore.

As we wrestled, the shark and I, a great crowd of people gathered, watching in amazement. After a very fatiguing struggle, I was able to drag the big fish onto the sand. A man from the watching crowd stabbed the shark to death with a pocketknife.

I staggered a few feet away and collapsed on the sand completely out of breath. In God's providence, a reporter was passing by the

Charles F. Weigle

area and noticed the great crowd gathered on the beach. Thinking someone must have drowned, he stopped his car to investigate. A bystander informed him that the man lying on the sand had brought in the man-eating shark with his bare hands.

The reporter stood over me and asked, 'Sir, is it true that you brought this shark in with your bare hands?' I told him, 'Yes it is true.' He said, 'That has never happened on this shore before.' I told him, 'As far as I am concerned–it will never happen again.'

Taking notes, the reporter recorded all the facts concerning my ministry, the special meetings and services and then took my picture. The next morning that newspaper that circulated throughout the main towns and communities along the coast carried the story of the evangelist who brought in a man-eating shark with his bare hands. My picture and the event were featured on the front page. That night the church was packed with people who had come to see the man they had read about in the newspaper. The Lord answered my prayer and filled the church–but in a very surprising way."

Some time ago while spending a night in Lafayette, Indiana, I remembered an event Charles Weigle had related to me–an event that had occurred in his childhood. "When I was a boy, our family lived in Lafayette, Indiana, near the old Wabash River. I was down under the old wooden City Bridge playing with some matches.

After a while the trash caught fire and was out of control in no time at all. Worst still the wooden poles and beams of the bridge were soon on fire. I ran home and hid in a small shed behind our house. Soon I heard the sound of sirens and firewagons. I asked my father what the noise was and he told me that someone had set the City Bridge on fire. I asked, 'What will they do to the person who did that?' He replied that they would lock him up in jail. 'What if it were a little boy?' My father said, 'They would lock him up too.' The entire bridge burnt down."

Years later Charles Weigle, then a well-known evangelist, held a meeting in Lafayette, Indiana. He found his way to the police station and told them that when he was a lad in the town that he

"That night the church was packed with people who had come to see the man they had read about in the newspaper. The Lord answered my prayer and filled the church–but in a very surprising way."

was the one who burnt down the City Bridge. The police laughed and said, "Well we needed a new bridge anyhow."

Charles Weigle wrote many songs which were published and sold widely. His most famous song was "No One Ever Cared For Me Like Jesus." With still a note of sadness in his voice, he explained how his first wife forsook him, betraying their marriage vows. After he had watched her and his daughter pull away on the train, he walked out on a pier extending out a ways into the ocean.

"I could hear the devil whisper, 'Weigle–jump into the water and all of your troubles will be over. End it all.'" After a moment of consideration he stepped back from the edge of the pier and said, "Satan you're a liar." In that moment God put something into his heart. Later, alone, forsaken, he wrote "No One Ever Cared For Me Like Jesus."

At 92 years of age, he told this writer that an estimated 20,000 people had come to Christ as a result of that song alone. Illustrating, he recounted: "In Chicago the newspapers carried the story of a man who worked in a lunch room. After being reprimanded, he returned to his place of work and killed a man. He was tried and sentenced to die in the electric chair.

Some Christians visited the man and led him to Christ. There was such a change in the man that everyone believed him to be sincere and truly converted. Intercession was made for him, but there was no reprieve. Again the papers carried the story. The condemned man walked the last mile to the electric chair singing…'No One Ever Cared For Me Like Jesus.'"

When the Communist regime fell in Romania, our mission organization set up various ministries in the country. Deep in the heart of Romania we attended a Romanian Church and heard a young woman sing in her native language "No One Ever Cared For Me Like Jesus." The song had pierced even the iron borders of communism.

Charles Weigle was 92 when he preached for us in our church. On the last night he preached on the title "A Trip To Heaven And Back." The sermon lasted over one hour and a half. The congregation sat at rapt attention almost spell-bound.

Some months later when word came to me of his death, I remembered his last words to me when I said goodbye at the airport: "James, one of these days you will get the word Old Weigle is gone. I just want you to know I will be in Heaven." His wonderful life had influenced thousands. His personal sorrows had only served to sweeten his spirit and to make him strength for others.

"I sing of Thee, and smile thro'tears

When sorrow comes to make me sad;

For I remember thro' the years

Thy grace, and sing because I'm glad.

I sing of Thee, O blessed Saviour,

Thy praise shall now my tongue employ;

I sing of Thee, O Lord, forever,

For Thou has filled my soul with joy."

- Charles F. Weigle

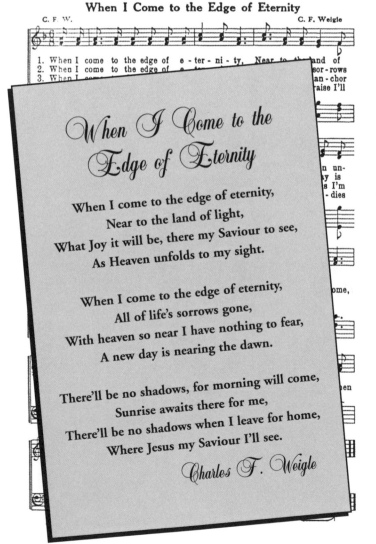

When I Come to the Edge of Eternity

C. F. W.   C. F. Weigle

1. When I come to the edge of e-ter-ni-ty, Near to the land of
2. When I come to the edge of
3. When I come

When I Come to the Edge of Eternity

When I come to the edge of eternity,
Near to the land of light,
What Joy it will be, there my Saviour to see,
As Heaven unfolds to my sight.

When I come to the edge of eternity,
All of life's sorrows gone,
With heaven so near I have nothing to fear,
A new day is nearing the dawn.

There'll be no shadows, for morning will come,
Sunrise awaits there for me,
There'll be no shadows when I leave for home,
Where Jesus my Saviour I'll see.

Charles F. Weigle

The Journey of

Adoniram Judson

The Experience of an Atheist
In a Country Inn!

THE sun had set and the darkness was settling in as the young atheist tied up his horse at a country inn. Tired from a day's journey, he stepped inside to inquire as to a room for the night. Apologetically, the landlord explained that only one room was vacant and that room was next door to the room of a man who was extremely ill and probably dying. The young atheist blurted out, "I'll take that room. Death holds no terror for me. You see, I'm an atheist."

The young man turned the key in his door with a feeling of pride. After all he was a college graduate with his own philosophy of life which excluded God. That night, however, the young man, Adoniram Judson, would discover that philosophies cannot answer the questions posed by impending death.

Judson unpacked his bags and endeavored to sleep, but sleep eluded him. The walls were very thin and all night he could hear clearly the groans and cries of despair coming from the next room.

Judson thought to himself, "The poor fellow is evidently dying in terror. I suppose I should go to his assistance,"

—but what could he say that would help him? He shivered at the very thought of going into the presence of the dying man. What hope would atheism offer a dying

Adoniram Judson had his own philosophy of life which excluded God. However, he discovered that philosophies cannot answer the questions posed by impending death.

man? Judson knew he could offer the man no hope, no peace or encouragement for atheism has none of these ingredients. All night long the dying agony continued. As Judson lay upon his bed, his life floated before him.

He had grown up in a Christian home. His father, a Congregational minister, had always prayed that his son would also one day preach the Gospel of Christ. Judson as a boy had displayed unusual abilities. He was only three years old when he learned to read under the tutelage of his mother.

As an older youth he was appalled at the thought of using his brilliance in such a dull occupation as the ministry. At the age of nineteen he graduated from Providence College as valedictorian. The pride of his heart gave him visions of being a great orator–perhaps a second Homer, writing immortal poems.

Judson was not only inordinately ambitious, he was also openly atheistic. It was during the early years of the 19th century, while Judson was in college, that French infidelity swept over the country. With only three or four exceptions, all the students of Yale were avowed infidels and preferred to call each other by the names of leading infidels, such as Tom Paine or Voltaire, instead of by their own names.

In the class just above that of Judson was a young man by the name of Ernest, who was exceptionally gifted, witty and clever. Earnest was also an outspoken atheist. An intimate friendship developed between these two brilliant young men, with the result that Judson also became a bold exponent of infidelity, to the extreme sadness of his father and mother.

Judson felt the presence of God beside him and the impelling call of missionary service. The road he was embarking upon would be a road of heartaches, tears and terrible persecution, but Adoniram Judson had heard the call of heaven.

When his father sought to argue with him, he quickly demonstrated his intellectual superiority, but he had no answer to his mother's tears and solemn warnings. The tears of his mother, the faith of his father, his spiritual rebellion, and now the cries of a soul nearing eternity in the next room all came down upon Adoniram's heart and mind. As he tried to compose himself, the dreadful cries from the next room continued.

He pulled the blankets over his head but still he heard the awful sounds– and shuddered. "How foolish he was," thought Adnoniram. "What would Ernest think of his thoughts?" Finally, all became quiet in the next room. At dawn, having had no sleep, he rose and inquired of the innkeeper concerning his fellow lodger. "He is dead!" "Dead!" replied Judson. "And do you know who he was?" "Yes," the innkeeper answered, "He was a graduate of Providence College." "Providence College, why that is the school of which I, myself, am a graduate. What was the fellow's name?" The innkeeper replied, "His name was Ernest."

Judson was overwhelmed by the news that the young man who died the previous night in the adjoining room in evident terror of death was his college friend Ernest, who had led him into

Adoniram Judson

During the months following the conversion of Judson, God placed upon Judson's heart the need of the world for the Gospel of Christ. There were others, like Ernest, who were without God and not prepared for death.

One day he felt a great need to pray and went into nearby woods. Falling down on his knees, he prayed: "More than all else, I long to please Thee, Lord. What wilt thou have me to do?" He immediately felt the presence of God beside him there in the woods and the impelling call of missionary service.

The road he was embarking upon would be a road of heartaches, tears and terrible persecution, but Adoniram Judson had heard the call of heaven. As with all great missionaries, there would be no power on earth to prevent him from answering. In the Baptist meeting house in Malden, Massachusetts, the traveler will find a marble tablet, bearing the following inscription:

infidelity. For many hours the words *Dead! Lost! Lost!* kept ringing in his ears.

Judson left the inn immediately and mounted his horse. His heartstrings pulled him toward home, toward Mother's tears and Father's faith. Turning his horse's direction, he rode toward home as fast as the horse would carry him. Arriving home, Judson begged his father and mother to help him find a faith that would stand the test of life and of death, of time and eternity. In one day the years of intellectualism and atheism crumbled before the saving power of Jesus Christ.

Rev. Adoniram Judson

Born Aug. 9, 1788

Died April 12, 1850

Malden, His Birthplace

The Ocean, His Sepulchre

Converted Burmans and

The Burman Bible, His Monument

His Record is on High.

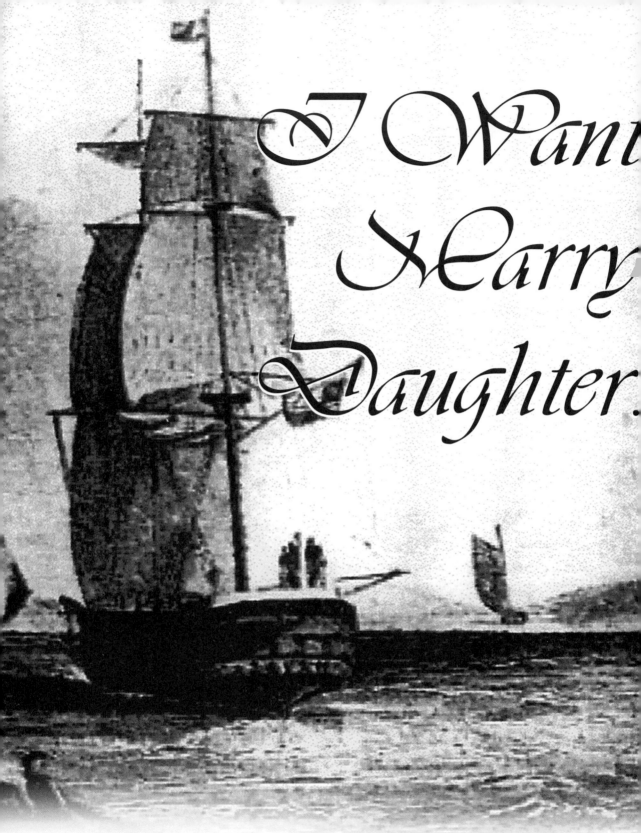

I Want Marry Daughter.

Adoniram and Ann were united in marriage in Feburary of 1812.
Just two weeks after their marriage, the happy couple left for the mission field.

To Your But...

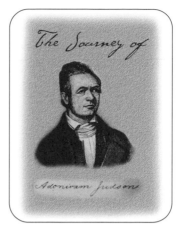

Adoniram Judson became convinced that Ann Hasseltine was the girl whom he was to marry. During the month that followed, he thought much about her and confirmed to himself the Lord's direction for marriage. Finally, he wrote her a letter and expressed to her his love and his desire to marry her. Ann wisely replied that he would have to ask permission of her parents before she would even consider the possibility of marrying him.

Immediately Adoniram sat down and wrote the following letter to Ann's father:

"I have now to ask, whether you can consent to part with your daughter early next spring, to see her no more in this world; whether you can consent to her departure, and her subjection to the hardships and sufferings of a missionary life; whether you can consent to her exposure to the dangers of the ocean; to the fatal influence of the southern climate of India; to every kind of want and distress; to degradation, insult, persecution, and perhaps a violent death.

Can you consent to all this, for the sake of Him who left His heavenly home, and died for her and for you; for the sake of perishing, immortal souls; for the sake of Zion, and the glory of God? Can you consent to all this, in hope of soon meeting your daughter in the world of glory, with the crown of righteousness, brightened with the acclamations of praise which shall redound to her Saviour from those saved, through her means, from eternal woe and despair?"

The father was obviously impressed with Adoniram's dedication and spiritual character. He would be happy for his daughter to marry such a man, but he left the final decision to Ann.

eanwhile, Ann's admiration and affection for Adoniram grew. After prayerful consideration she dedicated herself both to him and to his call. With the blessing of her father, Adoniram and Ann were united in marriage in February of 1812.

Just two weeks after their marriage, the happy couple left for the mission field.

Ann loved Adoniram with a love faithful unto death. Together they bore the reproach of Christ.

Samuel Newell and his bride Harriet sailed with them on the same ship. Luther Rice, Samuel and Roxana Nott, and others who had dedicated themselves as missionaries would follow as soon as they could raise their support.

Ann stood with Adoniram through deep waters. Beautiful stories of faithfulness and devotion are on record of Ann Judson. She suffered loneliness when Judson was in prison, disease of body and heartbreak of losing children in a foreign culture hostile to her very presence. Ann loved Adoniram with a love faithful unto death. Together they bore the reproach of Christ.

On one occasion Judson, pitifully weak and emaciated, was driven in chains across the burning tropical sands. With his back lacerated beneath the lash and his feet covered with blisters, he fell to the ground and prayed that the mercy of God might let him die. For almost two years he was incarcerated in a prison too vile to house animals. The stench of the place was terrible. Vermin crawled everywhere. He would have despaired of hope and ministry were it not for the beautiful encouragement and devotion of Ann.

Judson had been invited to accompany the British Commissioner on an envoy to Ava to negotiate a commercial treaty with the Burmese government. If he would accompany the Commissioner, he was promised the prize reward of religious liberty. (This was later refused.)

Adoniram and Ann kissed goodbye in the little house at Amherst and together they prayed. Everything seemed promising. During the journey a few weeks later Judson was handed a black sealed letter (emblem of grief) from a British officer. He went into his room, broke the seal and read,

"My Dear Sir: To one who has suffered so much, and with such fortitude, there needs but little preface to tell a tale of distress. Mrs. Judson is no more...

Ann had taken sick with fever and was DEAD. The letter continued,

The story of Ann Hasseltine Judson's faithfulness to her husband, Adoniram, and to her faith is unparalleled in missionary history.

"We have buried her near the spot where she first landed, and I put up a small rude fence around the grave."

Some weeks later, a broken-hearted man sat down in the desolate house at Amherst and wrote to the mother of Ann, back in America. Judson wrote:

Amherst, February 4, 1827

Amid the desolation that death made, I take up my pen once more to address the mother of my beloved Ann. I am sitting in the house she built, in the room where she breathed her last breath, and at a window from which I see the hopia tree that stands at the top of the small, rude fence which they have put up to protect it from incautious intrusion.

Mr. and Mrs. Wade are living in the house, having arrived here about a month after Ann's death; and Mrs. Wade has taken charge of my poor motherless Maria. Mrs. Wade met me at the landing-place, and as I passed on to the house one and another of the native Christians came out, and when they saw me they began to weep.

At length we reached the house, and I almost expected to see my love coming out to meet me, as usual. But no; I saw only in the arms of Mrs. Wade a poor little sick child, who could not recognize her weeping father and from whose infant mind had long erased all recollection of the mother who had loved her so much.

She turned away from me in alarm, and I, obliged to seek comfort elsewhere, found my way to the grave. But who ever obtained comfort there? Thence I went to the house in which I left her and looked at the spot where we last knelt in prayer and where we exchanged the parting kiss.

In the spring of that sad New Year, the child Maria, aged two years and three months, was laid by the side of her mother under the hopia tree, which shaded their graves with its fair name of hope.

Yes, so much had transpired since that holy day when Judson sat down to write Ann's father requesting the hand of his daughter in marriage. His letter had been prophetic. All that he had stated in that letter, the cost of his daughter to become a missionary to Burma, the pouring out of her life for others and for Christ, had all come to pass. *That happy union had been one long journey of tears.* Those tears would flow into rivers of living water, bringing with it a multitude of precious souls to Christ in a heathen land.

Adoniram Judson was one of five men to be ordained as the first American Foreign Missionaries to Asia in this service at the Tabernacle Church of Salem, Massachusetts. This has become one of America's most famous ordinations.

The Most Sacred Spot On Earth!

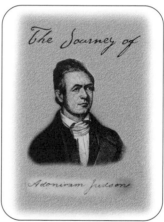

The Journey of

Adoniram Judson

The strings of his heart pulled him like a magnet into the Tabernacle Church in Salem, Massachusetts, where years before he, Adoniram Judson, had consecrated himself to missionary service.

This was his only furlough and visit back home after spending thirty-three years among the heathen in Burma. This spot was as sacred to him as Mecca was to a Moslem. How much that decision, thirty-three years ago, had cost him in the service for Christ.

Memories swept over Judson like a flood. The record states that he wept aloud. In

The Judsons sailed from this harbor at Salem, Massachusetts, in 1812 on the ship Caravan bound for Calcutta.

those very sacred moments he relived his life and past days. On Thursday, the sixth of February 1812, Judson knelt at this spot with Gordon Hall, Samuel Newell, Samuel Nott, and Luther Rice for ordination as one of the first missionaries from America to the unevangelized in Asia.

This has become one of America's most famous ordinations. The tabernacle was packed and even standing room was scarce. God was sending men to the unevangelized. America was becoming a missionary society.

On February 5th of that year Judson had taken lovely Ann Hasseltine as his bride. On the 19th of February Judson and Ann embarked on the sail ship *CARAVAN* bound for Calcutta. The reality of their decision to follow Christ soon replaced the missionary glory of their send-off.

The first trial came when Judson began studying the Scripture on this voyage in order to prove to William Carey (already on the field) that the Baptists were wrong on baptism. The result was that Judson became a Baptist before he reached Calcutta. This was a serious decision. He could no longer expect support from the churches that sent them out. Later Luther Rice returned to America to raise support among the Baptists.

After spending some time in India with William Carey at Serampore, the

The bench on which Judson and Luther Rice knelt at the Commissioning services at Salem

Judsons were forced to leave the country by the British East India Company. Carey recommended that they begin a work on the Isle of France. The Isle of France was a treacherous five thousand ocean miles away. Wherever the Judsons went, the British East India Company pursued with papers of deportation.

The company wanted no missionaries to interfere with their trade. In Madras the American missionaries were given notice to leave within two weeks. Adnoniram and Ann had vowed not to return to America. They now were ready to sail on any boat–anywhere–and wherever that boat took them would be their mission field. A boat was leaving before their legal deadline–a boat to BURMA.

The night before going on shore would be forever in Judson's heart. Ann was desperately

The Tabernacle Church where Adoniram consecrated himself to missionary service for Christ was as scared to him as Mecca was to a Moslem.

ill and had given birth to their first baby that soon died and had to be buried at sea.

The sound of pigs fighting for garbage in the streets continued through the night. Before them lay a squalid, unspeakably filthy village untouched by western influence. In a letter written by Judson a short while after this arrival, he stated that "this night was the most gloomy and distressing we have ever passed."

The next morning, July 13,1813, they disembarked. Mrs. Judson was so ill she had to be carried on a stretcher. The tears came again as Judson thought of Ann, faithful Ann, who thirty-three years ago stood with him at this altar at Old Salem Church.

The story of Ann's faithfulness is unparalleled in missionary history. She had married him only days before they set sail from U.S. shores for India. Through the rough sea voyage and uncertain landing on foreign shores Ann remained steadfast to their calling. She suffered loneliness when Judson was in prison, disease of body, heartbreak of losing children in a foreign culture hostile to her very presence. Ann loved Adoniram with a love faithful unto her early death. She died of fever while Adoniram was gone on a political trip to Ava for the Burmese goverment.

Yes so much had transpired since that holy day when Judson with the others knelt to be ordained as missionaries to the heathen. His missionary career had been one long journey of tears, but those tears would flow into rivers of living water bringing with it a multitude of precious souls to Christ in a heathen land. From this sacred spot Adoniram Judson turned again toward Burma to again suffer and finally to die for...

Jesus Christ!

royal love STORY

Sarah Ferguson and Prince Andrew

*On the day of the wedding,
I witnessed a love story far
greater than that which
took place in Westminster Abbey.*

July 23, 1986, will be forever engraved upon the walls of my mind. For weeks all of the British papers had been full of it, a love story. A trim young prince was to marry a beautiful red-headed young lady. Truly the wedding of Prince Andrew and Miss Sarah Ferguson was a Royal Love Story.

The day had arrived. Westminster Abbey was in readiness. The whole world watched by satellite. Literally millions of people were in London to catch a glimpse as the famous glass coach came rolling through the streets, headed toward the church with the royal bride.

The Bride arrived at the Abbey; the multitude gazed in wonder; the trumpets sounded out the news that the moment had arrived. With her father, Major Ronald Ferguson, the bride walked down the aisle on carpet that had never been trod upon before that day. The crowds were thrilled into a stunned silence as she joined Prince Andrew at the altar.

The choir began to sing scripture set to music:

*"Set me as a seal upon thine heart
As a seal upon thine arm;
For love is strong as death.
Many waters cannot quench love,
Neither can the floods drown it.
Set me as a seal upon thine heart
For love is strong as death."*

No, I can never forget the day of the wedding because…on the day of the wedding of Prince Andrew and Sarah Ferguson, I witnessed a love story far greater than that which took place in Westminster Abbey.

One Hundred miles to the north of London, I walked with an assembly of people up a gravel path through a gate to a church. The crowd was much smaller than that in London. The gate was not glittering with gold. The church was not decorated with gold and silver and freshly laid carpet like Westminster Abbey. It was a small stone building. There was no sound of singing or music or trumpets.

The chariot was not a magnificent glass vehicle but a wooden coffin, carrying the body of an American missionary wife to be planted in a lonely English cemetery. The missionary couple had served the Lord in Ethiopia. There she had lost her health in the harsh and bitter climate. Ethiopia had been a nerve shattering experience with the Communist Government takeover. From Ethiopia they had moved to Kenya.

Here, in another rugged environment, this couple had suffered robbery several times. On one occasion robbers had come into their home when they were there, beaten her husband, and threatened to rape her. They then stole her precious wedding bands. Now in England again they endeavored to serve the Lord. Two and a half years they had been here, about 15 miles from our city. What just days before had appeared to be a complete nervous breakdown turned out to be a tumor of the brain, and she was suddenly GONE. We bore her body at the very hour of the Royal Wedding in London to the lonely English grave. In a letter a few days later her brokenhearted husband penned these words:

At the very hour of the Royal Wedding in London, we bore the body of a loving missionary wife to the grave in a lonely English cemetery.

"In ETHIOPIA she lost her HEALTH
In KENYA she lost her WEDDING BANDS
In ENGLAND she lost her LIFE."

July 23, 1986, records all the pomp and ceremony in London with the Royal Wedding. Far away from the crowds of London in a rainy, windy, lonely spot, I stood in Stamford Cemetery and witnessed a LOVE STORY that those millions in London knew nothing about. I witnessed a LOVE STRONG AS DEATH.

The lonely scene was unknown and unnoticed by the millions in London but cherished by the God of Heaven.

"Set me as a seal upon thine heart, As a seal upon thine arm, for LOVE IS STRONG AS DEATH. Many waters cannot quence love for LOVE IS STRONG AS DEATH."

William Cowper
Poet Who Touched the World

Olney, England! Take away the modern signs, replace the road paving with cobblestone and the cars with carriages and you have left a village as it was 300 years ago.

The Cowper Tearoom in Olney is perhaps one of this writer's favorite places in the world. This quaint little place offers the atmosphere of old England. I love to go there. There I can sample the traditional English pastry, sip famous English tea from real china and glance across the street to the old home of William Cowper, the famous poet and writer of hymns.

There it seems I return to an era long gone. There I can almost hear the beats of the horses' hoofs as they pull the carriages along the cobblestones. When I sit there, the noisy world of the 20th century, with its information overload and avalanche of violence and moral decay, disappears into a world where men still *wrote* and *thought* and *believed*.

Olney brings me back to the Christ of *"Amazing Grace"* and the holiness of God. Again I walk with men who wrote mighty hymns exalting God in contrast with today's empty religious lyrics. William Cowper was perhaps the greatest poet and writer of hymns that ever lived. If not that, he surely takes his place in line with the Wesleys, Isaac Watts and Fanny Crosby. Unlike the shallowness of most of today's writers,

Cowper's hymns strike deep into the soul with a divine message from God.

When William Cowper was two days away from his sixth birthday, his mother, Ann Donne, died. Her death profoundly affected the young child. The Coopers lived in the rectory house in Great Berkhamstead. His father was chaplain to George II.

The weeping child heard the tolling of the church bells, announcing the funeral of his mother. Looking out the window, he watched the black horse-driven hearse slowly move from the house carrying his mother to the grave. Young William waved goodbye to the one he loved most and wondered where she had gone. Would he ever see her again? This tragedy affected William Cowper for life. His poetry reflected the impact of this sorrowful loss of his mother.

"I heard the bell toll'd on thy burial day,
I saw the hearse that bore thee slow away,
And, turning from my nurs'ry window, drew
A long, long sign, and wept a last adieu!"

The maids who tended young William were confounded when he would cry for his mother. They would promise him that she was coming back–someday. Cowper wrote:

"Thy maidens griev'd themselves at my concern,
Oft gave me promise of a quick return,
What ardently I wish'd I long believ'd,
And, disappointed still, was still deceiv'd;

William Cowper was perhaps
the greatest poet and writer
of hymns that ever lived.

By disappointment every day beguil'd, Dupe of to-morrow even from a child. Thus many a sad to-morrows came and went, Till, all my stock of infant sorrow spent, I learn'd at last submission to my lot; But, though I missed thee, ne'er forgot."

At night William missed the tender touch of his mother. Remembering his pain and her sweetness, he wrote: *"Thy nightly visit to my chamber made, That thou mightest know me safe and warmly laid."*

Sixty-three years later when William Cowper was sixty-nine years old, he

threatening. His mind wandered back to the only time in his life that he had known complete safety.

The old gentleman studied the forever-young picture of his mother. He mediated on every feature of her face, loving her, adoring her and remembering the gentle touch of so long ago.

"Oh, that those lips had language! Life has pass'd With me but roughly since I heard thee last, Those lips are thine—thy own sweet smile I see, The same that oft in childhood solaced me; Thy meek intelligence of those dear eyes Blest be the art that can immortalize."

The Cowper Tearoom in Olney is perhaps one of this writer's favorite places in the world. This quaint little place offers the atmosphere of old England, where you can sip famous English tea and see the Cowper House Museum across the street.

received a picture of his mother from a cousin in Norfolk. Memories flooded his mind. The years had been traumatic and

Soon after his mother's death, Cowper was sent to a boarding school in the nearby village of Market Street. The little boy, grappling with the death of his mother, now had to experience the absence of his father in a strange place. One of the older boys bullied young William into a complete state of terror. Years later William recalled the experience in complete detail.

Cowper later attended Westminster, then one of the foremost public schools in England. Westminster was the school for the children of noted families. Here he excelled in the classics and general academics. When he left Westminster, he could write as easily in Latin as he could in English.

At eighteen Cowper became the apprentice to an attorney and in 1754 was called to the Bar. Two years later he was appointed to the post of Commissioner of Bankrupts with a salary of £60 a year.

In 1750 William had met Theodora, his cousin, at her father's house in Southampton Row. They fell in love and were for a time engaged to be married. Marriage to cousins was acceptable and considered completely appropriate in those days. Laws forbidding close kinship marriage came into being much later with the enlightenment of medical statistics. Theodora's mother opposed the engagement, and the marriage plans were abandoned. Theodora remained his benefactor for life.

Cowper's early years passed with general youthful happiness. He entertained himself with his ex-Westminster friends,

who had formed a group called the Nonsense Club. Members of the group contributed light writings to periodicals that were in publication at the time. Cowper published five articles.

That life-style came to an abrupt end in 1763 when Cowper was 32 years old. There is no clear explanation as to what happened to Cowper's health in 1763. He became very melancholic and at times greatly depressed. Some writers have suggested that he could not stand the pressures of his law profession. Many causes have been suggested, such as psychological, religious, neurological, physiological and even nutritional.[1] No one can speak with absolute certainly.

Modern terminology would describe Cowper's dilemma as a "complete nervous breakdown." Underneath the happy, carefree face of William Cowper was a storm ready to break. The breaking point came when he faced an examination before a public panel as a candidate for the Clerkship of the Journals for the House of Lords.

Underneath the happy, carefree face of William Cowper was a storm ready to break. The death of his mother, the brutal treatment in his early school days, and the upcoming examination now all met in one emotional moment.

The examination loomed over him like the incoming clouds of a storm. As the date drew near, the pressure increased. Now the seeds of all of William Cowper's fears and insecurities germinated. The death of his mother, the brutal treatment in his early school days, and the upcoming examination now all met in one emotional moment.

Cowper had reached the breaking point and attempted to take his life.

Gratefully the attempt failed. For the following eighteen months (1763-1765), he was confined to a mental hospital in St. Albans. Under the kind attention of Dr. Nathanael Cotton, an evangelical believer, Cowper began his journey back.

t was a beautiful morning in July of 1764 when Cowper picked up a Bible and began reading from Romans. Nick Rhodes in his book describes the event:[2]

"Suddenly, for the first time in many months, he began to experience an in-rush of hope, an almost hysterical joy. This was, in true Evangelical tradition, the moment of his conversion, the turning-point in his life."

Cowper had lived a moral and an honorable life. His father had been a minister. His mother had been an honorable, righteous woman. All of his life had been, in a sense, "religious," but until this moment there had been no personal experience.

From this moment onward, Cowper was a new man. His world changed and he changed the world. However, he was a damaged man. Still at times he would be plunged into despondency.

Often he needed assurance and council. He struggled between the extreme Calvinism of Whitefield and the reality and assurance of personal faith. Inside of the great man was a doctrine that said, "You might be cursed and damned as the non-elect" and another voice of personal faith and experience. In all probability William Cowper's problem was physical and emotional which translated into religious doubts.

God sent along helpers. In 1765 he settled in Huntingdon with the family of a minister, Reverend Morley Unwin. Soon afterward Mr. Unwin was killed from a fall from a horse. When the Unwins and Cowper moved to Olney in 1774, they were visited by the Rev. John Newton. John Newton was a great help to Cowper and a calming, assuring voice in his life when he needed it most.

Together they published the "Olney Hymns," containing some of the greatest hymns ever written. Of these hymns 280 were written

All of Cowper's life had been, in a sense, "religious," but until one morning in July of 1764 there had been no personal experience.

by Newton and 68 by Cowper. Newton's hymns include the following:

"How Sweet The Name Of Jesus Sounds,"
"Glorious Things Of Thee Are Spoken,"
"May The Grace Of Christ Our Saviour,"
"Amazing Grace, How Sweet The Sound."

Among those written by William Cowper are the following:

"O For A Closer Walk With God,"
"Hark My Soul It Is The Lord,"
"God Moves In A Mysterious Way,"
"Jesus, Where'er Thy People Meet,"
"There Is A Fountain Filled With Blood."

The publication of the "Olney Hymns" propelled Cowper into fame. His influence, along with Newton's, spread throughout

Great Britain into the vast commonwealth of Nations including America.

Some writers have portrayed William Cowper as a madman—who wrote great hymns and died in despair. This writer feels that this does great injustice to one of the greatest men who ever lived.

Cowper suffered tragedy at six years old with the death of his mother and fought a deep emotional depression in the second half of his life. During those periods he seemly lost assurance when that condition plunged him into depression. The reader should separate the "ill Cowper" from the Cowper who wrote with such conviction and depth in normal conditions.

John Newton and his wife Mary had great affection for Cowper.

The hymn "God Moves in a Mysterious Way" has been a source of great comfort and blessing to many of God's people since William Cowper wrote it in the 18th century. Yet few people know of the unusual circumstances that led to its composition.

William Cowper was a Christian, but he had sunk to the depths of despair. One foggy night he called for a horse-drawn carriage and asked to be taken to the London Bridge on the Thames River. He was so overcome by depression that he intended to commit suicide. But after two hours of driving through the mist, Cowper's coachman reluctantly confessed that he was lost.

Disgusted by the delay, Cowper left the carriage and decided to find the London Bridge on foot. After walking only a short distance though, he discovered that he was at his own doorstep! The carriage had been going in circles. Immediately he recognized the restraining hand of God in it all.

Convicted by the Holy Spirit, he realized that the way out of his troubles was to look to God, not to jump into the river. As he cast his burden on the Savior, his heart was comforted. With gratitude he sat down and penned these reassuring words:

"God moves in a mysterious way
His wonders to perform;
He plants His footsteps in the sea,
and rides upon the storm.
O fearful saints, fresh courage take,
the clouds you so much dread
Are big with mercy, and shall break in
blessings on your head."

As I sat in the old Cowper Tearoom across from his home, I thought of the words of one of his hymns. Feeling that he had strayed from Christ,

Cowper wrote:

"Where is the blessedness I knew
When first I saw the Lord?
Where is the soul-refreshing view?
Of Jesus, and his word?
What peaceful hours I once enjoy'd!
How sweet their mem'ry still!
But they have left an aching void,
The world can never fill.
Return, O holy Dove, return,
Sweet messenger of rest;
I hate the sins that made thee mourn,
And drove thee from my breast.
The dearest idol I have known,
Whate'er that idol be;
Help me to tear it from thy throne,
And worship only thee."

People in Cowper's era read poetry. For one hundred years after his death, Cowper was a household name in England. He has been regarded as one of England's greatest poets.

Often when Cowper was gripped by depression, he came to the Vicarage for help from his pastor, John Newton. Both John Newton and his wife Mary had great affection for "Sir Cowper." When Newton left Olney for London in 1780, it was a great blow to Cowper. Still he had Mrs. Unwin, who had been like a mother to him.

In 1796 Mrs. Unwin died and Cowper was left alone. The gloom returned and four years later he died. Cowper was a great man–a great man "propped up" by those whom God put in his path. There had been Dr. Nathanael Cotton, the Unwin Family, and John Newton. All of these had calmed William Cowper in his hours of need.

Did Cowper have assurance of his salvation? Yes! Did he have doubts in fits of depression and sickness? Yes! This writer is certain that William was saved and that in normal and ordinary times he had great assurance based on his experience and the Word of God. After all…we too must hold to the promises and not to OUR feelings that come and go.

Read again the great hymn "There is a Fountain" and feel the assurance that gripped Cowper's soul. NO ONE–

For centuries the poems of William Cowper have lifted the hearts of condemned men to God. Through that noble writer of hymns, throngs of souls in conflict have found assurance and peace.

NO ONE–could write such words without assurance, even if later that assurance was mislaid during times of depression.

"There is a fountain filled with blood
Drawn from Immanuel's veins,
And sinners plunged beneath that flood
Lose all their guilty stains.
The dying thief rejoiced to see
That fountain in his day,
And there may I, though vile as he,
Wash all my sins away.
E'er since by faith I saw the stream
Thy flowing wounds supply,

Redeeming love has been my theme
And shall be till I die.
When this poor lisping, stammering tongue
Lies silent in the grave,
Then in a nobler, sweeter song,
I'll sing Thy power to save."

A few months before his death, William Cowper, looking at his mother's picture, penned *"I shall meet thee on that peaceful shore."*

April 25, 1800, at the age of 69, William Cowper lay down to die. John Newton recalled:

"About half an hour before his death, his face, which had been wearing a sad and hopeless expression, suddenly lighted up with a look of wonder and inexpressible delight. It was as through he saw his Saviour. Those who attended his funeral, at which John Newton preached, said that this look of wonder remained even as he lay in his coffin." [3]

The "poor lisping stammering tongue" lay silent in the grave–yet for centuries since, that tongue has lifted the hearts of condemned men to God. Through that noble writer of hymns, throngs of souls in conflict have found assurance and peace. Perhaps dear reader…YOU should go to Olney and VISIT the Cowper Tearoom. Sit there with a cup of English tea, meditate and say with William Cowper…

"The dearest idol I have known,
Whate'er that idol be;
Help me to tear it from thy throne,
And worship only…Thee."

"And Satan trembles when he sees
The weakest saint upon his knees."

- William Cowper

Anne Donne Cowper, mother of William Cowper
The sorrowful loss of William's mother when he was only
6 years old would affect him for life and impact his poetry.

[1] William Cowper, *Selected Poem,* Nick Rhodes, Carcanet Press Ltd., Manchester, England.
[2] Ibid.
[3] *Favorite Men Hymn Writers,* Jane Smith & Betty Carlson, Crossway Books, Wheaton, Il.

The Old Cornerstone

W e had parked in front of the old Dixon Printing Company in Kettering, England, when my wife noticed it first. She called my attention to the cornerstone of the old building which read: *"This Stone laid by Rev. William Booth."*

The building had once served as a church. William Booth had been there. He had preached in that very building. When the building was dedicated, he had laid with his own hands the cornerstone in place. Sometime later, parking in the same location, I discovered the building had been demolished and reduced to a pile of rubble and broken stones. Somewhere in that pile of rock and debris was the treasured cornerstone. In vain I searched for it.

William Booth was a legend. Because he dared to notice people for whom no one else cared–the world noticed him. He stepped out of oblivion on to a world stage, bringing with him the poor and desolate, drunkards and harlots and the unloved and unsought. Booth was a "nobody" who cared for "nobodies." He valued men's souls as worthy of redemption. I would have treasured that cornerstone had I found it in the rubble. I would have placed it on

The Story of William Booth, founder of the Salvation Army

the grounds of my home to remind me to care for men and women without Christ.

When other eyes viewed a human race with scorn and disdain, his eyes saw "apples of gold in pictures of silver" (Proverbs 25:2). The American Civil War was in its final stages when William Booth began his work in England in 1865. Booth with Catherine, his wife, was embarking on a work that promised only sacrifice and hardship. That work would propel them into an area of public disdain initially.

William was born April 1,1829, of Church of England parents. His baptism occurred two days later. His mother was a devout Christian woman. His father, Samuel, had accumulated a good deal of money but through misfortune lost it. His advice to his son William before he died in 1842 was to "make money." He accepted Christ on his deathbed. Samuel Booth died bankrupt.[1] The death of his father changed everything economically for William and his mother. Plunged into immediate poverty, William was forced to seek employment although he was only 13.

That same year, William became an apprentice to a pawnbroker. Work hours extended some days to 16 hours a day. The pay was very low. This limited his opportunity for a former education. He did receive help from a private tutor.

Booth broke with the Church of England and began attending Wesley Chapel of Nottingham. He was converted in 1844 at the age of 15. The impulse to serve God came to him when an American evangelist, James Caughey, preached in Nottingham. Greatly impressed, Booth began his own ministry of reaching out to men. His first attempt at preaching was on street locations.

Unfortunately, the men Booth most wanted to reach threw bricks at him and mocked his message. Undaunted, the young preacher sought out some poor, ragged boys from the slums. The pastor rebuked him and instructed him to bring them through the back door. The boys were to be seated in a section of the church where they would not be noticed by the more respected members.

Bricks thrown during street services were one thing but opposition from his own minister was astounding. This was his first warning that he might have to reach beyond the borders of the religious establishment if he wanted to reach the lowest of the low.

By 1852 Booth was preaching in various churches in London and the midlands. That same year he accepted a Methodist circuit at Spalding. While ministering in this area, he met Catherine Mumford. He stated that he fell in love with her the third time he saw her, which was on Good Friday April 10. The couple was married June 16, 1855, in South London.

By the time of his wedding, Booth had become a well-known preacher. Every meeting he held brought hundreds of converts to Christ. The Isle of Guernsey was selected as their honeymoon spot. There they would be away from it all for that special occasion. When they arrived, however, a great crowd of people met them on the pier, pleading with them to conduct a revival meeting. They could not resist. Ed Reese in his work on Booth states: *"The crowds were so large the doors had to be opened at 5:30 in order to allow the people to come in for the evening service. He was soon preaching in England's leading cities… London, Bristol, Bradford, Manchester, Sheffield and thousands professed faith in Christ."*[2]

The Methodist leaders intent on quieting Booth down withdrew him from evangelism and assigned him to a small out of the way circuit. In 1861 at age 32, William Booth resigned his position with the Methodists and entered independent evangelism. He began his new ministry in Cornwall.

At Hayle, Cornwall, the crowds were so large no building could be found to accommodate them. The meetings were held in the open air. Seven thousand Cornishmen were converted. In Staffordshire five thousand others responded to the call of Christ.

William and Catherine began the Salvation Army July 2, 1865. That decision propelled the couple into a different ministry arena. Booth preached in saloons, stables, sheds, warehouses, backstreets and anywhere that people would listen. His workers were bitten, beaten and some killed. Their clothes were torn and their band instruments destroyed. Salvation Army marches ended in riots. An army of thugs would disrupt the meetings and wreck the building. Owners sometimes refused to rent halls. Police often refused protection. *The Watchword*, Volume 24, describes Booth's troubles: "When spit on

during the Midlands tour, Booth encouraged his fellow soldiers, "Don't rub it off—it's a medal." Night after night Booth would come home bleeding and bruised after being attacked for preaching in the slums of England.[3]

In this context William Booth needed a bodyguard. Peter Monk, an Irish prizefighter converted under Booth, volunteered. Despite the trouble, Booth would not give up. By 1899 there were 81 stations and 127 full-time evangelists. The group conducted 7,500 services a year.

In the years that followed, Booth organized the movement in other countries including America. He preached from New York to Kansas City, holding crowds spellbound. In 1890 he published a book entitled *Darkest England and the Way Out.*

"Some men have a passion for art. Some men have a passion for fame and gold. I have a passion for souls."

The book was a best seller. Booth's ministry now included social services to the destitute as well as a spiritual emphasis.

By 1891 the man had become a legend. Twice he opened the American Senate in prayer. Once he spent 20 minutes with President McKinley. Great men praised him, including Charles Spurgeon, Winston Churchill and King Edward VII. When asked by King Edward what his recreations were, Booth replied, "Sir, some men have a passion for art. Some men have a passion for fame and gold. I have a passion for souls."

Once William Booth was asked the secret of his success. His answer:

"I will tell you the secret, God has had all there was of me. There have been men with greater brains than me, men with great opportunities. But from the day I got the poor of London on my heart and caught a vision of all Jesus Christ could do with them, on that day I made up my mind that God would have all of William Booth there was." [4]

William Booth died on August 20, 1912. Catherine, his faithful partner and loving wife, had died several years before. London streets were crowded for nine miles and 10,000 people attended her funeral. As William Booth lay in state at the huge exhibition hall in London, up to 150,000 people passed by his body. Forty thousand attended the funeral—one of them Queen Mary. The Queen sat next to an ex-prostitute—a convert of William Booth.

In his life he had traveled more than five million miles reaching out to others. The man who had dared to notice those the world would not notice was now noticed by kings and queens, statesmen, and presidents.

Toward the end of his life, he was scheduled to speak at a great convention. The hour arrived and the thousands had gathered to hear the old soldier, but he had not arrived. Finally an announcer stood to tell the great crowd that General Booth was ill and would not be able to attend the convention—but he had sent a message—a telegram. Carefully the

Abney Park

speaker opened the telegram to find that it contained only one word…the word—*"OTHERS."* – signed William Booth.

The driver of the great machine that knocked down the old Dixon Printing Company that day in Kettering, England, saw nothing of value in the debris. Without a thought, he smashed to rubble the old cornerstone laid by Booth.

I would have cherished it!!

[1] The on-line magazine of *St. Peter's Church, Nottingham.*
[2] *A Great Cloud of Witnesses,* p.15, Dr. Ed Reese, Faith Baptist Church Publications.
[3] *The Watchword,* volume 24.
[4] *A Great Cloud of Witnesses,* p. 20, Ed Reese, Faith Baptist Publications.

The Lonely Man on...
The Banks of the Thames

William Tyndale gave his life for the Bible. In London, England, his monument stands on the banks of the Thames River with "Book in hand." One wonders what he would think today of the commercialization of the Bible and the irreverent handling of the Word of Truth.

It was in Belgium that the author completed the last phase of a journey following the footsteps of WILLIAM TYNDALE. At various times along the way and in different locations, there had been the footprints... of William Tyndale.

Those footprints had appeared in Bristol, England, on the banks of the Thames in London, in Worms, Germany, and now at last in Belgium where it all ended. The year was 1535, October 6. Tyndale was taken from prison, tied to a stake on the spot where the author stood and strangled. His body was burned to ashes.

Of course it is not accurate to state that it all ended there. The flames that engulfed this man of God were only the beginning of Tyndale's work. Ironically, even my very presence on that spot was a continuation of Tyndale's work...of spreading the Word of God.

William Tyndale was born in the year 1484 in the county of Gloucester, England. Very little is known of his childhood. Our first historical notice of him in 1512 was after he had graduated from the University of Oxford. After this he went to Cambridge, where it is most likely he met Hugh Latimer. In 1520 when Tyndale was 36 years old, he accepted the post of Chaplain to Sir John Walsh's household and tutor to his children. Here at the Manor House in Little Sodbury, Tyndale sojourned for three years. His bedroom has today been furnished with old-world furniture, making it look

William Tyndale 1492 - 1536

Mighty Man of the Bible!

In his life, Tyndale translated the entire New Testament and portions of the Old Testament.

similar to when he actually occupied it. The preacher ministered in a nearby church and publicly preached in nearby Bristol where he was arrested. The charge against him: "SPREADING HERESY IN AND ABOUT THE TOWN OF BRISTOL."

On occasions church dignitaries were invited to the manor house at Sodbury. During conversations at dinner, the names of Luther and Erasmus came up. One of the clerical guests asserted that people were

woman could read the Gospels; that they might be translated into all languages so that the husbandman should sing portions of them to himself as he follows the plough; that the weaver should hum them to the tune of the shuttle, and that the traveler should beguile with their stories the weariness of his journey."

Tyndale now saw the possibility of bringing the dream to reality. Finding publication in England impossible, he fled to Hamburg in 1524. Some of Tyndale's friends who

The Manor House - Little Sodbury, England, where Tyndale lived for three years

"better without God's laws than without the Pope's." Tyndale made a defiant reply. With blazing conviction and burning eyes, he replied, "If God spare my life, ere many years I will cause a boy that driveth the plough to know more of the Scripture than thou doest."

The writings of Erasmus greatly influenced Tyndale. Erasmus had published a New Testament for the benefit of the more learned classes, but Greek and Latin were of little use to common people. Erasmus had stated: *"He wished that even the weakest*

had helped in London were arrested and punished. It is believed that Tyndale visited Martin Luther in Wittenberg.

Tyndale was brilliant, having a wonderful knowledge of language. He was so proficient in German, Dutch, Italian and Spanish that whichever he might be speaking, the hearer would think it to be his native tongue. In 1525 a translation of Matthew and Mark was being printed by Tyndale at Cologne. This was stopped by an injunction by the dean of Frankfurt. When one door closed behind him, he opened another. The translator moved to Worms, where he completed printing of 3,000 New Testaments which were smuggled into England. William Tyndale had the ability to work at tremendous pace, perhaps sensing a shortness of time and life for his work. Today in Britain there is a major alert at ports of entry for drugs. The alert in 1526 was for BIBLES. The East Coast ports—London, Yarmouth, King's Lynn and Hull—were all being watched for the coming of the objectionable book.

Spies had been busy for a long season. It became necessary to change the type, size and style of book in order to outwit the authorities. Bibles were hidden in wrappings, cases and crates of all kind. The "smugglers" had wonderful success. More than half the people of England seemed eager to read, and Tyndale's Scriptures filtered out to the population.

Young men went from city to city selling the precious Word. Some paid dearly with their lives for this crime. In desperation the Bishop of London embarked on a scheme to "buy up" all the incoming Bibles and then destroy them. A shipper, who favored Tyndale, cooperated with the plan. Tyndale received enough money from the sale to print twice as many Bibles as the Bishop received. God moves in mysterious ways His wonders to perform. The Bishop of London was financing the very book he wanted most to destroy.

It was on the 11th of February in the year 1526 that the great public burning of Bibles took place. The pile consisted mostly of Tyndale's works but included some of Wycliffe's Bibles and Luther's works. Meanwhile in the "Land of Reformation" the translator pressed ahead with his life's work. He was a man with one idea in life —to do the will of God and to publish His Word.

Tyndale had made this statement about the year 1520 to the clergyman: "If God spare my life, ere many years I will cause a boy that driveth the plough to know more of the Scripture than thou doeth." Some mere 15 years later he had translated the entire New Testament and

A castle once stood near the spot where William Tyndale was burned.

portions of the Old. Thousands of copies were being smuggled into England.

He was a man of action. In midsummer 1534 he was staying at the home of a friend in Antwerp. The Papal spies were constantly following his tracks and knew where he was. However, as the law stood, he could not be arrested while he resided in the home of an Englishman. At last Tyndale was deceived by another Englishman who lured him out of the house to dine where he was arrested. Taken to a Castle at Vilvorde, 18 miles from Antwerp, he was imprisoned in a vile cell. The cells in those days were damp, dark windowless dungeons.

He asked the governor of the Castle to permit him the use of a candle in the evenings, as well as his Hebrew Bible and some other books. He also requested that he might have his cloak to stave off the chills. October 6, 1536, he was led out to be burned. It was all over…or was it?

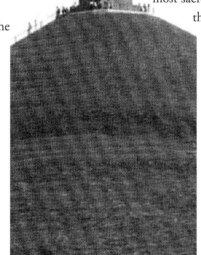

Waterloo—where Wellington defeated Napoleon in 1815

Some 30 miles from this site is another famous monument at Waterloo. This location is where the Duke of Wellington defeated Napoleon Bonaparte in a history changing conflict. The event marked one of the greatest battles of European history. After the battle of Waterloo, all of England was greatly concerned about the outcome. Had Wellington lost? Would Napoleon rule over England? In those days there was no telegraph, no telephones or radio to bring the news.

The outcome was wigwagged by semaphore. The watchers high on the tower spelled out the words. Soon the message came in.

"W-e-l-l-i-n-g-t-o-n   d-e-f-e-a-t-e-d"

At that moment a dense fog settled over the channel and the semaphore could no longer be seen. The sad heartbreaking news broke over the city. Later the fog lifted, the semaphore was visible and the complete message was spelled out.

"W-e-l-l-i-n-g-t-o-n d-f-e-a-t-e-d t-h-e E-n-e-m-y!"

Now the city rang with joy. There are two great monuments in Belgium: one is hardly known, seldom seen and never publicized, yet it marks the greatest and surely the most sacred spot in Belgium. When the enemies of the Word of God lit the fire to burn the translator, they publicized the tidings

"JESUS DEFEATED– NO MORE BIBLES– TYNDALE IS DEAD."

However, through time the mist has lifted and the true message flashes out the news "THE WORD OF GOD IS VICTORIOUS."

Millions and millions of Bibles have been printed in the common tongue. The printing presses roll on. On the banks of the Thames stands a lonely figure with the "Book" in hand. Let Christians take the "Book" in hand and press on with the news. The time is short. The need is for men to be men of action. Let us not rest until all the world has heard. "HOW BEAUTIFUL ARE THE FEET OF THEM…that bring glad tidings of good things…so then faith cometh by hearing and hearing by the WORD OF GOD." (Romans 10:15,17KJV)

The Man From Scotland

Who Left His Heart In Africa

"Nothing earthly will make me give up my work in despair.

I encourage myself in the Lord my God and go forward."

- From the diary of David Livingstone

Livingstone's Home at Blantyre, Scotland

"Friends, I have forgotten all I had to say." With those words the young missionary candidate to China left the pulpit and rushed out of the church, leaving his congregation in a wondering stare. The directors of the London Missionary Society hearing of this account decided that this young man would never make a missionary. The young man, David Livingstone, would have been dismissed on the spot if one of the directors had not spoken up in his favor and persuaded the others to give him a second chance.

Having been given a second chance, David Livingstone gained approval of the missionary society and was fully accepted as a missionary candidate. Livingstone prepared himself thoroughly for his work. He prepared himself by studying medicine as well as by studying theology.

His original desire had been to serve God as a missionary to China. However, China became closed to missions during this period of time due to the "Opium War." The directors of the mission then suggested to Livingstone that he go to the West Indies as a missionary. Livingstone felt that serving in the West Indies would be too much like serving at home.

His heart was already considering the vast continent of Africa when by chance he met Robert Moffat, one of the best known missionaries of that day. Moffat was home on leave when one day Livingstone asked him if he thought he would "do for Africa." Moffat replied in words that became the guiding rule for the rest of David Livingstone's life, "You will do for Africa, if you do not go to an old station, but advance toward unoccupied ground. In the north I have sometimes seen, in the morning sun, the smoke of a thousand villages, where no missionary has ever been."

David Livingstone's heart from that moment on belonged to Africa. It was God who had spoken to Livingstone's heart through the lips of Robert Moffat. On December 8, 1840, he sailed in the *George* for South Africa.

The Africa that Livingstone found was for the most part an unknown world. To the European mind, it was a dark and mysterious continent. Europeans were fascinated by this land of pygmies and giants and cannibals and subterranean rivers. Africa to the world at large was a mere outline. Very little was known of the interior beyond the coastal settlements.

David Livingstone spent his life exploring the dark continent, plodding deep into the interior where no white man had ever been and even crossing the continent. His goal was to open up the continent for the Gospel of Christ. Livingstone saw much of death during his life. He witnessed the murder of hundreds of Africans by the slave traders.

He worked constantly against the slave traders and accomplished much towards having slavery outlawed. Countless times Livingston's life was in danger. His philosophy toward his danger was summed up in his statement: "A man seems almost immortal until his work is done!"

On one of his journeys, his wife, the daughter of Robert Moffat, died of a jungle disease and had to be buried along the trail. The trail through Africa became for David Livingstone a trail of tears, sickness, frustration and many times despair, but still he plodded on, driven by the will of God to open up Africa for the Gospel.

Deep in the heart of Africa, still plodding on but sick unto death, he wrote in his diary: "Nothing earthly will make me give up my work in despair. I encourage myself in the Lord my God and go forward." On April 29, 1874, they reached a village where they found accommodations in an empty hut, offered by a friendly chief.

It was apparent that Livingstone could not be moved and so they left him in bed. His faithful servants, Susi and Chuma,

Dr. Livingstone's medical bag

cared for him hourly. In the early hours of the morning of May 1, David Livingstone crawled from his bed to kneel and pray. His wife dead, his people thousands of miles away, his body in pain in a dark heathen hut in the heart of unknown Africa, Livingstone slipped out of his earthly body and ascended to glory.

His servants found him dead beside the bed, still kneeling. They cut his heart from his body and buried it there on the spot. They then carried his body to the coast to British authorities to be carried to England for burial. For almost 1500 miles, they fought their way through hostile tribes with that body, never allowing it to touch the ground; so much they reverenced their master.

David Livingstone died as alone as any man could die. We know, however, from his testimony that he never really felt alone. When speaking to a group in Britain, he had said that the abiding presence of Christ was the one thing that kept him going.

When Livingstone had first embarked on his journey to Africa, some friends had accompanied him to the ship. One friend in particular had encouraged him not to go. To this friend he turned and said, "Jesus said, 'Go ye therefore, and teach all nations whatsoever I have commanded you: and, lo, I am with you alway, even unto the end of the world.'" Then Livingstone said, "And that, sir, is the word of a gentleman."

Some years ago on my first trip to London, I visited Westminster Abbey in London. In the middle of that giant cathedral, I stood at the grave of David Livingston. I thought of all that he went through in Africa. I thought of his wife dying there and his hardships. One question loomed in my mind: "Why? Why would a man go through all of that? What could possibly motivate a life of suffering like that?"

Several years later I found the answer to the question of Westminster Abbey. I was in Scotland visiting the homeplace of Livingston. I saw the bed he slept in as a boy. I looked at the tools he worked with in a nearby mill from early morning until after dark. I read the actual letters that he had written. Then I saw it–his motto as a young man–the theme of his life. As a young man Livingstone had picked up a pen and had written: "I WILL PLACE NO VALUE ON ANYTHING THAT I HAVE OR POSSESS EXCEPT AS IT RELATES TO THE KINGDOM OF CHRIST."

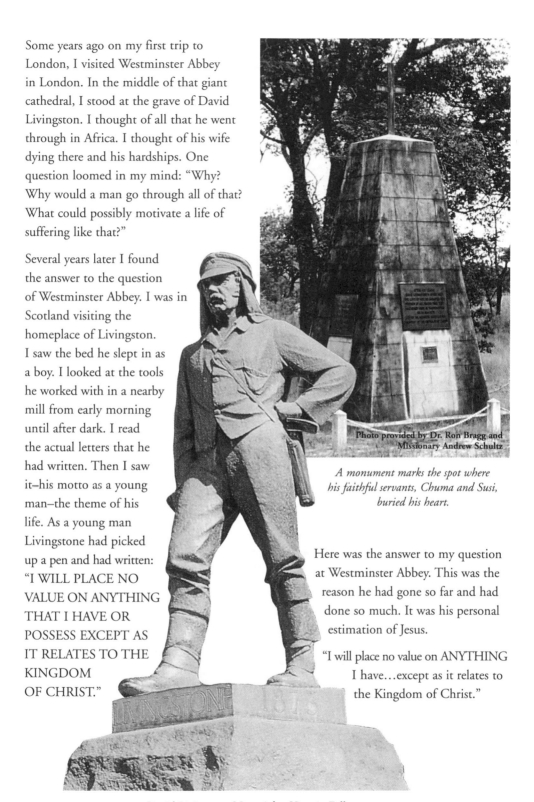

Photo provided by Dr. Ron Bragg and Missionary Andrew Schultz

A monument marks the spot where his faithful servants, Chuma and Susi, buried his heart.

Here was the answer to my question at Westminster Abbey. This was the reason he had gone so far and had done so much. It was his personal estimation of Jesus.

"I will place no value on ANYTHING I have…except as it relates to the Kingdom of Christ."

David Livingstone Memorial at Victoria Falls

Robert Livingstone yearned for the approval of his world famous father, Dr. David Livingstone.

The Solemn Secret
of Salisbury, North Carolina

Beneath a beautiful grassy plot of land in the cemetery at Salisbury lies the body of Rupert Vincent. Vincent's body lies in an unmarked grave along with thousands of Federal army soldiers who died at the Salisbury Prison camp during the Civil War. This large unmarked area has the appearance of a pleasant park amidst surrounding fields of tombstones and markers.

The grim reality, however, is that this immaculate piece of sod hides the bodies of thousands of unknown young men who never made it home. One name among the unknown fallen, however, survives–the name of Rupert Vincent.

When Vincent's body was laid to rest at this spot among a thousand other dead, the field did not have the appearance of a garden. It was a rugged, dirty trench. Here, mixed with the dirt, mud, and blood, lay shattered hopes, unfulfilled dreams, and loving hearts of youth… now, all ended by the grief of war.

Salisbury Prison, an old factory, was the major Confederate prison in North Carolina and at one time held some 15,000 men. During the early stage of the conflict, conditions were relatively good. When Rupert Vincent arrived in October of 1864, the overcrowding had begun.

By November, an area that could accommodate 1,200 to 2,000 for a short period of time held almost 9,000. Ten to twenty-five prisoners were buried daily. One building was designated as the "dead house."

"When I see Dad again–

maybe–just maybe he will say,

'Son, I am proud of you.'"

Rupert Vincent was a long way from home. Salisbury's confederate prison was a bewildering location for an eighteen-year-old Scottish lad. Just two years before, his mother died in Africa.

The Salisbury Prison, where Livingstone was held

He missed her. Now in the wretched conditions of a prison camp, he thought of her warmth and gentleness.

His father, a missionary in Africa, thought him a failure. Rupert thought, *"I wonder what he would think of me now–here a prisoner in this place. Perhaps Dad would think, 'I knew he would end up like this.'–if only I could make him proud, if only I could be like Him."*

The young man yearned for the approval and acceptance of his world famous missionary father– Dr. David Livingstone. Perhaps he thought, "When I see Dad again– maybe–just maybe he will say, 'Son, I am proud of you.'" In the stern and rigid way 19th century British parents reared children, words like these were seldom spoken.

A lonely house, surviving by the old railroad, witnessed the sorrow and grief of days long gone.

Rupert Vincent, in reality Robert Livingstone, was born during one of his father's African expeditions in 1845. His mother, Mary, was the daughter of another famous African missionary, Robert Moffat. David and Mary had high hopes for their little son. This was reflected in their naming him "Robert Moffat Livingstone."

The year was 1852 when Mary returned to England with the children. During this time, they lived a life bordering on poverty.

Robert was seven years old and showed signs of being strong-willed. Being away from the discipline of a father, he developed a personality of early independence.

Until his father's return in 1856, he had shared his mother's poor existence, moving from room to room and town to town. At the age of twelve, young Robert was sent to a series of boarding schools in Scotland and North England. Because of behavior problems, his father wrote stern letters, commanding him to end his "vagabond ways."

Stern letters, however, did not calm the restless spirit of Robert Livingstone. Born in Africa and having lived on a mission station with his father gone much of his short life, the lad felt a sense of not belonging anywhere.

In 1858, Mary joined her husband in Africa. After being reunited for only three months, Mary died of a fever at Shupanga. On her deathbed in Africa, she worried about Robert and the children in Scotland. Knowing that death was near, Livingstone kissed her.

Lying with her mouth a little open, she gently shut it and breathed her last breath. The man who had faced so many deaths and braved so many dangers wept like a child. For the last ten years of her life, Mary had no settled home in which to bring up the children. Now she was gone.

Livingstone turned his attention to his children. Writing a loving letter to each of them, he penned, "With many tears running down my cheeks I have to tell you that Mama died last night at seven o'clock… She loved you dearly and often talked about you… You must all love each other more than ever now."

Robert's difficulties with adjustment continued. With his mother dead and never really knowing his father, he felt frustrated. At the age of eighteen, he announced that he was not prepared to submit to any further education. Livingstone felt that Robert, by not furthering his education, would limit himself to manual labor. At times he had accused him of being lazy. Livingstone, in a letter to his son Thomas, expressed the possibility that Robert was only interested in making capital out of having a famous father.

Robert asked his father if he could travel to Zambesi to talk with him about his future. Perhaps some sort of apprenticeship could be worked out. This request was really a son's craving to be with a father he had never known. Mother was dead. The world was a lonely place for Robert. Perhaps, he must have thought, "We can talk and be together." In Africa where he had been born, the family, mother, father and children, had all been one—and home had been "home."

The trustees of the mission made provision for Robert's journey to Africa but thought nothing of the funds he needed to go inland to his father. His father had told a friend that if he saw Robert, to tell him that he would have to work his way out.

His father was fighting the slave traffic in Africa. This would be his chance to do the same. This act reflected a deep respect for his father and a longing to be like him. Perhaps this would be his chance to prove worthy of acceptance of a father he little knew.

Mary Moffat, Robert's grandmother, was sick with worry after hearing about his situation.

After returning to Africa in 1863, Robert never met with his father. Being unable to locate his father, he found employment on an American ship and sailed for America in the late summer of 1863. The ship landed at Boston, and Robert enlisted with the 3rd Regiment of New Hampshire on October 3, 1863.

His father was fighting the slave traffic in Africa. This would be his chance to do the same. This act reflected a deep respect for his father and a longing to be like him. Perhaps this would be his chance to prove worthy of acceptance of a father he little knew.

From the end of 1863 until he returned to England in the summer of 1864, David Livingstone heard nothing from Robert. Then in July, a letter arrived from America. It was a moving letter. Robert addressed his father as "My dear Sir." The letter revealed a young man who was growing up. Robert expressed regret that he had thrown away his chances of education.

The letter from a field hospital in Virginia continued, "I have changed my name for I am convinced that to bear your name here would lead to further dishonor it." These words must surely have pierced David's heart. Robert went on to describe two skirmishes: *"I never hurt anyone knowingly in battle, have always fired high. In that furious madness which*

The field of unmarked graves containing the bodies of thousands of Civil War soliers, including the son of David Livington, the famous missionary

*always accompanies a bayonet charge
which seems to possess every soldier,
I controlled my passion and took the
man who surrendered prisoner."*

He then signed the letter with the
name of Rupert Vincent. Dr. Livingstone
received his son's letter in England, where
he was on furlough. Not long afterward
he met, almost by chance, the American
ambassador to England, Charles Francis
Adams. Ambassador Adams agreed to
make inquiries about Robert. Finally,
Dr. Livingstone was informed in a letter
dated December 17 that Robert had been
captured by the Confederates.

After falling into the hands of the
Confederates on October 5, 1864,
Robert Livingstone began his final
journey, which would lead to Salisbury
Prison. At Salisbury, conditions became
desperate as prisoners poured into
the compound. Food supplies ran so
short that some prisoners caught and
roasted rats.

During a food riot, guards fired
into the crowd of prisoners.
Robert Livingstone, who was
not thought to be involved, was hit by
fire. According to old hospital records,
twenty-three wounded prisoners were
admitted to the hospital on the Monday
of the riot. One of those prisoners was
named Rupert Vincent.

In December 1864, the son of Dr. David
Livingstone died in a prison camp in
Salisbury, North Carolina. What were
his final thoughts? Perhaps his suffering
mind wandered back to Africa, to England,
to Mother…to Dad. Would he ever be
proud? Would he ever know?

David Livingstone still did not know
about Robert's death in June of 1865.
He wrote, "Robert we shall never hear
of again I fear…but the Lord is merciful
and just. He would hear the cry for
mercy in the hospital at Salisbury."

What David Livingstone had accomplished for Christ was immeasurable.
The cost had been staggering. His family
could not have survived had they been
with him in Africa. Had he stayed with
them in Britain, the work of Christ would
have suffered. The slave trade would have
continued to damn millions of people to
untold suffering and misery. Yet, on the
human side–there was Mary in her grave
and Robert. Six years later when Henry
Stanley found David Livingstone in
Africa, he told him of the death of his
son. Stanley was the last white man to
see Livingstone alive. Livingstone was
fighting the hated slave trade in Africa
and his son had only tried in his own
way to "be like his dad," who fought to
set slaves free.

Livingstone's heart was grieved. With
all the encouragement he had given to
the world, he had neglected to encourage
his son. In his efforts to direct Robert
away from error, he had been blinded
to his real qualities. Now he saw himself
repeated in Robert.

Robert had dared to take the road
less traveled. As recorded in his diary,
Livingstone uttered words long overdue,
words of praise and esteem, words for
Robert, words whose syllables, too late,
fell upon lifeless ears, "If I had been there,
I would have gone to fight also…I AM
PROUD OF YOU SON."

"I can plod!"

-William Carey

William Carey —
God's Plodder!

he old town of Kettering in England has experienced centuries of history. In the hundreds of years the city has existed, famous people have walked the streets and lived in the town. **William Booth** preached there. **John Gill** lived there. **Kings** have passed through the city. Perhaps the most sacred spot in Kettering is the home of a widow affectionately known as "Widow Wallis."

Living only five miles away, I would see the old Wallace Home almost every week. It never ceased to inspire me, knowing what happened there. The Wallis Family were active members of Fuller Baptist Church. There was so much church activity in their home that it was nicknamed "The Gospel Inn." It was here in the home of Widow Wallis that the first mission board was organized.

On the 2nd of October 1792, in Widow Wallis's parlor, twelve ministers, one deacon and one student established "The Baptist Society for the Propagation of the Gospel among the Heathen," the springboard of the modern missionary movement. A collection taken in Andrew Fuller's snuffbox raised £13 2s. 6p.–a considerable sum in view of the poverty of most of those present.

The student who signed himself "Anon" on the list of donors and who borrowed his 1016p., repaying it from preaching fees, was William Staughton. Immigrating to the United States, he founded the American Baptist Missionary Convention, serving as its secretary and president until his death. He is reported to have said that the "fire of missionary enterprise was lit within him in Widow Wallis's back parlor."

William Carey was born in Northhamptonshire the 17th of August 1761 in the tiny country village of Paulers Pury. This was a time when the British Empire was expanding its power across the world, a time which demanded great men. These were exciting times. In the American colonies George Washington was ready to lead America in a war of

Carey Mission House, Kettering, England

worked, he began language study. On his own, without a teacher, he mastered Greek, Latin, Dutch and French.

In time, Carey was commissioned to preach by the company of Baptists at Olney and became part-time minister of the church at Moulton. After moving to Moulton in 1785, he ran a small school, tended his shoe trade and pastored the church next door. He would bring his finished shoes to Thomas Gotch, his employer and encourager at Chesham House, who sold them and supplied Carey with a fresh quantity of leather for further work.

In this small cobbler's shop Carey made shoes while looking out the shop window at a village of 300 people, but seeing beyond them the millions perishing in other lands. This vision ultimately led to the *"Deathless Sermon of Nottingham"* in May of 1792.

The meeting was held at Friar Lane Baptist Church. William Carey was scheduled to preach at 10:00. Little could anyone present know, including Carey himself, that he was about to change the world forever. His sermon would become famous as *"William Carey's Deathless Sermon,"* because it initiated a movement that lives forever. Opening his Bible, he preached

independence. John Newton was fighting the slave trade. John Wesley was setting the whole country ablaze with the Gospel.

*I*n England, there was a Mr. Grant who had come from India to try to persuade the Archbishop of Canterbury to start a mission in the colony. The Archbishop presented the request to the King of England but the king refused. He wanted no new religions to be introduced into India which might disturb the new colony. The archbishop and the king closed the door on missions to India. At that point God moved around the throne of England and the established religious system. He began a new work in an obscure village in the heart of the English countryside with the birth of *William Carey.*

Apprenticed to a shoemaker, he was converted through the witness of a fellow apprentice, a dissenter called John Warr, and attended the Hackleton Meeting House. In the shoe shop where he from Isaiah 54:2: *"Enlarge the place of thy tent…stretch forth the curtains of thine habitations, lengthen thy cords and strengthen thy stakes."* The sermon was entitled **"EXPECT GREAT THINGS FROM GOD–ATTEMPT GREAT THINGS FOR GOD."**

It must be remembered that the ministers in the meeting were mostly, like Carey, pastors of small, poor village churches with congregations numbering in some case no more than twenty-five members. Also this meeting represented only one small group in the various associations that made up the Baptist movement of that day.

*A*nother serious consideration of the times was the paralysis of extreme Calvinism. The often vocal and common opposition to evangelism of heathen lands was the persuasion that if God wanted the heathen saved, He would do it without human help. In a previous meeting Carey had been rebuked by an older man when he attempted to discuss the Great Commission.

At this meeting in Nottingham, however, Carey would not be silenced. He poured out his heart for those in spiritual darkness. He was preaching for a verdict. This sermon demanded action. In the business meeting that followed, routine matters were discussed but not a word about missions. Carey's heart burned within him. When the chairman asked if there were any new business, Carey turned to Andrew Fuller sitting next to him. Gripping Fuller's arm, he said, *"Is nothing again going to be done?"*

Andrew Fuller was a leading influence among local Baptist circles. When he became involved in Carey's vision for

missions, things began to happen. Before the meeting adjourned, it had been resolved to present a plan for a Baptist Mission Society when the next ministers' meeting was held in October at Fuller's church in Kettering.

Carey's touching appeal led to the historic meeting in Widow Wallis's parlor on the 2nd of October 1792. After the day's services were over, the twelve ministers gathered in a back room of Widow Wallis's home. The plan for a mission board was presented. Let it be emphasized again that the majority of these preachers were from small area churches. They could not know how much their simple decisions would eventually mean to the world. God, however, was beginning a work through them far beyond their own

The ministers who founded the first Baptist Mission Board were like Carey, pastors of small, poor village churches with congregations numbering in some case no more than twenty-five members.

understanding. This author has seen and held the original minutes of the meeting of October 1792.

Looking down the list of names of twelve ministers, including Andrew Fuller, John Sutcliff and William Carey, my eyes locked on the bottom of the page. There was totaled the offering, *the first offering given by Baptist churches as a group for world*

In the small English village of Kettering were planted the tiny seeds of modern day missions with twelve Baptist ministers and £13.20s ($50.00).

missions. The sum total was £13.20s, amounting to probably $50 in today's money. There in the small English village of Kettering were planted the tiny seeds of modern day missions with twelve Baptist ministers and £13.20s. From this small beginning has come millions and millions of dollars for missions, along with thousands of missionaries who for two hundred years have covered this world winning souls for Jesus Christ. It could have so easily failed to materialize.

There were many obstacles. England would not grant a work permit; thus, English ship captains refused to issue tickets. The mission society had raised only about three hundred pounds. The passage was six hundred pounds. There was vocal opposition and scorn from extreme Calvinists. Carey visited John Newton, the converted slave trader and author of *"Amazing Grace,"* for advice. John Newton told him, *"If God is in it no power on earth can hinder you."*

On March 20, 1793, the mission board met and set apart Carey and another missionary for service abroad. Andrew Fuller said on that occasion, *"There is a gold mine in India, but it seems as deep as the center of the earth."* Carey replied, *"I will venture down into that mine to dig, but remember* **YOU MUST HOLD THE ROPES."**

What emerged on that momentous occasion in Leicester was a consensus by the home pastors and churches that they would stand by the missionaries until **DEATH**.

June 13, 1793, leaving England on a foreign ship and still without a work permit, the Careys set their eyes toward an unknown horizon. They had very little money to sustain them upon their arrival in India. The journey was rugged, taking five months without one time putting into port.

After being in India for a short time, the Carey's five-year-old son caught a fever and died. After his death, Mrs. Carey became very depressed. The depression grew into mental illness. After being in India for eight years, she had completely lost her mind and soon died.

Carey's sister wrote of him, *"Whatever he began he always finished."* Carey once described himself as a plodder. It was a just self-evaluation. *He plodded* when he had no money or ship to take him to India. *He plodded* when he had to work full time in India to support his family. *He plodded* when extreme Calvinists rebuked him for wanting to convert the heathen.

When his loving little son died, *he plodded*. When his wife, depressed by all the tragedy and hardship, lost her mind, *he plodded*. When she died, *he plodded*. He later remarked when his second wife died after thirteen years of happy marriage, *"My loss is irreparable. I am very lonely."* Still Carey plodded on with the Word of God. For over forty years, without a single furlough, HE PLODDED. HE WAS GOD'S PLODDER!

At sunrise on June 9, 1834, in Serampore, India, William Carey died. Sometime ago I visited Regents College, Oxford, England, and stood beside the couch on which he died. The couch had been sent to England to be preserved for the Baptist archives. Looking down, I tried to visualize Carey in his final moments. Had it made any difference to anyone that he had lived? *"He had expected great things from God. He had attempted great things for God."*

When he arrived in India, only two small provinces had a portion of Scripture. Only two small lights were burning. When he lay down on that couch to die, he had translated all or part of the Bible

For over forty years, without a single furlough, HE PLODDED. HE WAS GOD'S PLODDER!

into thirty-four Indian languages. Almost all of India at least had access to the printed Gospel.

Churches had been established and native preachers were preaching. Serampore College had been established and he had started the modern-day missionary movement. The door was open for others to follow. Adoniram Judson followed. Hudson Taylor followed. Robert Moffat followed. David Livingstone and thousands of others followed.

Carey's cobbler shop still exists in the village of Moulton, England, a village that has changed little in two hundred years. Positioned in a corner of the little room is the pulpit from which Carey poured out his soul to the church next door. There is the bench where he sat making shoes and studying languages, looking out the window at a dull village of perhaps three hundred people but **SEEING THE WORLD.**

Just a village…just a shoe cobbler… but **LITTLE IS MUCH WHEN GOD IS IN IT.** Dear Friend, will you expect great things from God? Will you attempt great things for God?

The "*Deathless Sermon of Nottingham*" lives on and will as long as there are men and women who, like Carey, have a heart for perishing souls in other lands.

"Expect Great Things From God!

Attempt Great Things For God!"

Daniel Marshall -
Baptist Legend!

Pioneer of the first Baptist Church in Georgia

On May 9, 1784, John Ray, of the author's ancestry, died at the age of sixty-seven. He had come a long way since his birth in Virginia in 1717. When Joseph Ray, his son, carried John Ray's body down to the grave, he was burying an American patriot. This man had been a great American revolutionary fighter but more than that *a great Christian leader.* Joseph would miss his counsel and prayers. Appling, Georgia, would be a lonelier place without his presence.

Then in November of the same year, Joseph again made his way out to the pioneer burial ground in the little village. This time, in sight of the old meeting house of Kiokee Baptist Church, he said goodbye to his pastor, *Daniel Marshall.* Two of the

greatest men that Joseph had ever known had vanished from the earth in one year… but their footprints would be seen for centuries in the Baptist movement in Georgia.

Daniel Marshall, the pastor of Joseph and John Ray, was a legend. After starting a string of churches in other colonies, Marshall moved to the Georgia Wilderness about thirteen miles west of Augusta, Georgia, and settled on Kiokee Creek.

There were no Baptist churches in the territory and he was the sole Baptist preacher. Soon he had organized services with a few families, and the group expanded as families whom Marshall knew in North Carolina and Virginia moved into the area. These new families included the Rays, Evans, Newmans, and Castleberrys.

DANIEL MARSHALL

BORN IN WINDSOR, CONN. 1706.
CONGREGATIONALIST WHO BECAME
SEPARATE BAPTIST DURING GREAT
AWAKENING. ORDAINED, ABBOTTS CREEK,
N. C. 1757. LEADER IN ESTABLISHING BAPTIST
WORK IN VIRGINIA, THE CAROLINAS, AND
GEORGIA. SUPPORTED CAUSE OF RELIGIOUS
LIBERTY; ARRESTED FOR PREACHING IN
GEORGIA. LED IN ESTABLISHING GEORGIA'S
FIRST CONTINUING BAPTIST CHURCH ON
THE LITTLE KIOKEE IN 1772. ONLY PASTOR
TO REMAIN IN GEORGIA THROUGHOUT THE
REVOLUTION. HELPED TO FORM GEORGIA
BAPTIST ASSOCIATION, FIRST IN STATE,
SHORTLY BEFORE HIS DEATH, NOV. 2, 1784.
GEORGIA BAPTISTS ARE INDEBTED TO HIM
FOR NURTURING MANY MEN WHO
CONTRIBUTED TO THE MOVEMENT'S EARLY
GROWTH.

Recently discovered site of Daniel Marshall's cabin on the banks of the Kiokee

Joseph would have been there by the creek when it happened. He would never forget what he saw. He would tell the story to his children and grandchildren. They would pass it on until the process of time faded it from memory with distant generations.

The church had gathered on the banks of the Kiokee for a worship service. Daniel Marshall had bowed on his knees to the ground to open the service in prayer. As the great preacher prayed, he felt a hand laid on his shoulder and heard a voice that said, "You are my prisoner."

Looking up, he recognized the officer of the law as Constable Samuel Cartledge. The constable informed him that he had violated the legislative enactment of 1758. This act established religious worship in the colony to be held according to the rites and ceremonies of the Church of England.

The preacher was ordered to appear in court in Augusta on the following Monday. If he gave a security deposit to guarantee his appearance, he would not be taken into custody on the spot. Abraham Marshall, in his work published in the *Analytical Repository* in 1802, confirmed that the arrested preacher was made to give security for his appearance in court before he could continue the service.

A few feet away, his wife, Martha Marshall, had witnessed the whole scene.

Colonial days were rugged days. Daniel Marshall thundered across the scene with a message from God. He was a man for his times.

She stood to her feet and denounced the arrest. This was America. This was not England. How could a law be right that would allow the arrest of a preacher of the Gospel? Quoting scripture to sustain her position, she spoke with such utter conviction that the constable himself was convicted. The words of Martha Marshall eventually led to his conversion.

In 1777, Constable Samuel Cartledge was baptized by the very man he had arrested and had led to court on the following Monday. For some years he served as a deacon for Daniel Marshall at Kiokee Baptist Church. In 1789, five years after Marshall's death, Cartledge was ordained by Abraham Marshall (Daniel Marshall's son) as a Baptist minister. The constable who arrested the preacher at Kiokee for preaching…became a preacher himself and preached for more than a half century.

The following Monday, Daniel Marshall appeared in Augusta for trial. After the proceedings had ended, he was ordered to "come, as a preacher no more into Georgia." The reply of Daniel Marshall was equal to that of the Apostles under similar circumstances, "Whether it be right to obey GOD or man, judge ye." Marshall continued his defense with the same bold assurance that he was right to preach the Gospel of Christ. The presiding judge was Colonel Barnard. Records indicate that Barnard was afterward converted and became a zealous Christian, although (in deference to the wishes of his wife) he was never immersed and remained in the Church of England. Barnard became a decided friend of the Baptists and spoke of them very favorably to Sir James Wright, the Governor.

Daniel Marshall remained in Georgia throughout the Revolutionary War when others had fled. He lived a life of conviction. It was this holy boldness and courage when handling truth that drew men like John and Joseph Ray to him. Colonial days were rugged days. Life was hard and dangers existed in every direction. Daniel Marshall thundered across the scene with a message from God. He was a man for his times.

The Baptist movement in Georgia would in time become worldwide, but its humble roots would always be found at Kiokee.

The Baptist movement in Georgia would in time become worldwide, but its humble roots would always be found at Kiokee. Out of that mother church would rise thousands of Baptist churches in Georgia. Out of those thousands of churches would come changed lives and strong families. From those families would come men and women who would change Georgia and who would make the world a better place.

On November 2, 1784, the seventy-eight-year-old pastor of Kiokee Baptist Church lay down to die. The *Analytical Repository*, in an article written by his son, records his last words with his wife sitting beside him:

"I am almost gone. I will probably die tonight. God has shown me that He is my God and I am His son. I have fought a good fight. I have finished my course… eternal glory is before us."

Joseph Ray was a witness to the will of Daniel Marshall. He was also appointed as one of the appraisers of his estate. Daniel Marshall wanted his wife, Martha, to be cared for. If there were anyone on earth he could trust for that sacred task…it would be Joseph Ray.

Joseph not only appraised and witnessed the will of Daniel Marshall, but he had been…

witness to a…Legend!

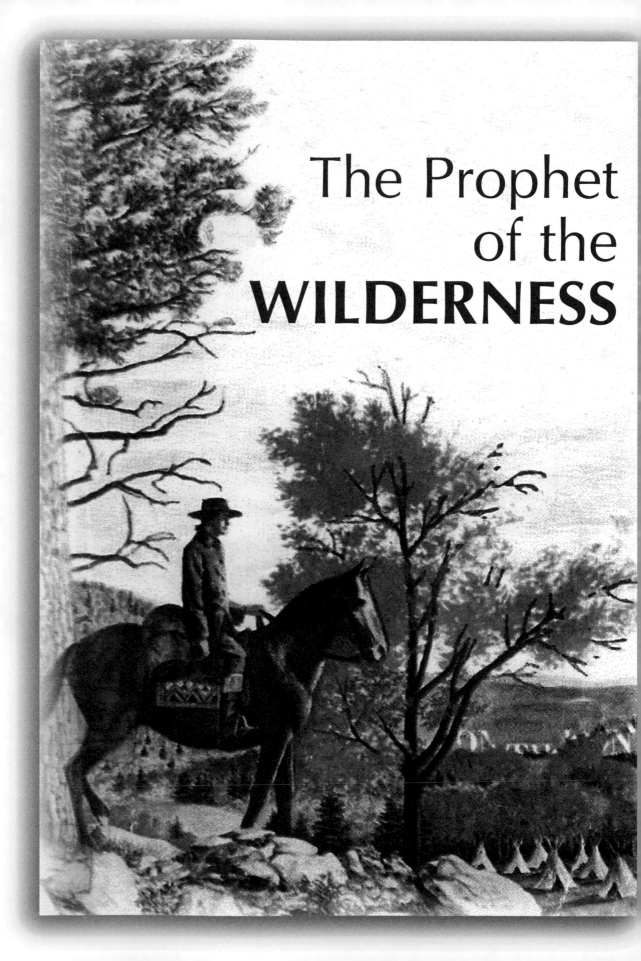

The Prophet
of the
WILDERNESS

**M**URDER was in the hearts of several red men who stalked the palefaced and frail young man as he ventured farther into the wilderness known as the "Forks of the Delaware." This territory had a well-deserved reputation for its danger and death. Tribes in the area had come to despise the white man because of his double-dealing, land stealing, and vices connected with whiskey and greed. Now another paleface coming into their woods inspired vengeance. David Brainerd, the frail young paleface, would probably prove to be the greatest friend the Indians would ever have.

Arriving at sunset and seeing the village campfires, Brainerd decided to spend the night in the nearby forest and approach the village the next day.

The Indians who followed, seeing the white man make a camp, departed to report to the village. The chief and warriors of the village decided to go out and kill the intruder that night. As they approached his camp, they were surprised to see him down upon his knees, praying fervently that God would save the Indians. They could not kill a praying man. They would wait. Hours passed, and the warriors grew weary of waiting. Still the white man knelt and prayed, pouring out his soul for the Indians. As he prayed, all eyes in the group were transfixed on a rattlesnake which made its way into his presence, lifting its poisonous head near the white man as if to strike.

Suddenly, without apparent explanation, it slithered past the missionary and into

"I love to live on the brink of eternity."

- David Brainerd

the night. The chief and his men, moved by the seeming protection of God on this stranger, also disappeared into the night. As they withdrew from the scene, the words of the praying paleface faded into the distant darkness, but the echo remained embedded deeply in their minds.

The next day as Brainerd preached in their village, one of the warriors, who had the night before intended to kill him, remarked, "This paleface is a praying man." Another said, "And the Great Spirit is with him." The chief's squaw commented, "And he brings a wonderful, sweet message."

David Brainerd was described by F.W. Boreham as "a man in a million." His story is one of the most moving accounts ever written of a man who wanted to live only for God and His will. David Brainerd was born at Haddam, Connecticut, April 20, 1718, and died on October 9, 1747, at the age of 29.

His life was one of hardship and trial and often of discouragement as he plodded on through the wilderness of early America, caring about the people that time forgot.

The reader must remember that these were the days of the 1700's, preceding even the birthday of America in 1776. Only about two million people lived in the colonies.

Brainerd faced many trials in his ministry. Often he slept on the ground, in the woods, or in the open with a little shelter, enduring winter cold and severe storms. The American Indians had grown weary of the white man who had deceived and swindled them of

Road Sign of David Brainerd

although he used every method and tool at his disposal, it was obviously not the tools being blessed but the Lord working on His own. After one meeting an Indian told Brainerd, "I want God to change my heart." Another stated that she wanted to find this Christ. An old man who had once been a chief wept bitterly over his soul. Indian men who had been murderers and drunkards came to Christ. After one service an Indian woman lay on the ground praying and crying, "Guttummaukalummeh wechaumeh Kmeleh Ndah," that is, "Have mercy on me, and help me to give You my heart." Others came to Brainerd saying, "I want Christ to wipe my heart clean." Unlike former days when Brainerd preached, tears now formed in the Indians' eyes. Brainerd noted that almost as soon as Indians arrived for the meetings, they were seized by the Spirit of God. In his diary for August 8, 1745, he wrote:

"I perceived under much concern, the power of God seemed to descend upon the assembly 'like a rushing mighty wind,' and with an astonishing energy bore down all before it. I stood amazed at the influence that seized the audience…like the irresistible force of a mighty torrent, or swelling deluge, that… sweeps before it whatever is in the way."

God was at work among the American Indians. When Brainerd departed to go to another area, the Indians commenced a

their homeland. It took several years for Brainerd to break down the natural prejudice which existed among the Indians against the white man.

During these years Brainerd prayed his way through. At first, he could not speak the language of the Indian tribes, but in spite of this he preached and prayed anyway, often in the power of God. Frequently discouraged and feeling himself a failure, Brainerd plodded on, telling the story of Christ to tribe after tribe.

About the year 1745, things began to happen. Brainerd wrote in his diary that prayer meeting for him which lasted from sundown until the next morning. Once Brainerd asked an Indian believer why he cried, and he replied, "When I thought how Christ was slain like a Lamb, and shed His blood for sinners, I could not help crying when I was all alone."

Again, the success of David Brainerd among the Indians could not be attributed to methods. Brainerd said, "God appeared to work entirely alone, and I saw no room to attribute any part of this work to any created arm." Perhaps the secret of God's power on Brainerd could be traced back a few years to his prayer life. He had come to the place in his life where God was all in all. He had turned away from the world and worldly honor to honor God alone. **Pleasing God alone was now the sole motivation of his heart.** He records in his diary during those early days:

"Oh, that I could live in the secret of God's presence."

Brainerd's memoirs reveal his constant hunger for God, his passionate desire for total devotion, and his yearning for Christlikeness. He wrote: *"O that my soul might never offer any dead or cold services to my God."* Beware of getting as close to God as did Brainerd; for God may love you so much He will bring you home early.

A trembling hand held the letter from the American Colonies as the director of the Scottish Missionary Society met to consider news from their missionary to the Indians: **"David Brainerd, your missionary is dead at 29."**

If only Brainerd had lived longer, so much more could have been done. BUT—so

much more WAS done! John Wesley read the **Life of Brainerd** and was fired with missionary zeal. William Carey read the **Life of Brainerd** and went to India. Henry Martyn read the **Life of Brainerd** and became a bundle of fire in the darkness of India and Persia. Robert MeCheyne read the **Life of Brainerd** and became an Apostle to the Jews. And now dear reader, *"What will your decision be?"*

Brainerd's life could have been different. The church at East Hampton called Brainerd to be their pastor. East Hampton was a pleasant little community described by Jonathan Edwards as one of the "fairest towns on the whole island with the church parish being the largest and most wealthy."

This church sought Brainerd as their pastor for a long time even before he had settled on his call to be a missionary. David's brother John settled into the civilized work in the cities of New England. John Brainerd was always the man on hand for the committees and appointments of the established situations. Had David only taken care of himself, he might have lived to a good old age–like John. For many years there was a little white slab on a little church at Deerfield, New Jersey, which read:

> *Here*
> *Under this Building*
> *is buried*
> *John Brainerd*
> **A BROTHER OF DAVID**
> *He was one time Pastor*

Church founded by David Brainerd, Belvedere, NJ (Photo by Rev. Glen Foster)

The Two Great Loves

of David Brainerd!

David Brainerd would never forget the first time he saw her. She had ridden down from Northampton with her father, Rev. Jonathan Edwards, who was to deliver the Yale commencement of 1741. Jonathan Edwards' sermon was wonderful, but his daughter was magnificent. Like her mother, Sarah, Jerusha was beautiful. Jerusha and David did not become acquainted that day, but their eyes met. Later, they officially met, and David Brainerd formed the habit of calling at the Northampton parsonage. One afternoon in October of 1743, the young couple talked. Jerusha confided to David that God had called her to become a missionary to the Indians. She added, "Father is giving me a course of study on 'The missionary wife.'"

Now thoughts of serving God together and winning the Indians to Christ filled their minds and hearts. It had to be. This was surely the plan of God.

In the months that followed, David Brainerd met with the leaders of the Scottish Missionary Society, was accepted, and began making more definite plans for his work. In January of 1743, Brainerd made his way to Long Island where he was to meet with the Society. A vicious blizzard blew during the entire 50 miles. Feeling faint, David thought, "If I become a missionary to the Indians, this will be my life in the wilderness…Can I endure? Should I go back now?"

For some time the snow beat against his face as he plodded on through the storm. Then in a moment of time the victory came, and he shouted, **"Oh GOD, I CHOOSE TO GO RATHER THAN TO STAY."** At 9:00 a.m. on March 25, 1743, Brainerd left New York City, riding toward the wilderness. Ahead of him was nothing but suffering, hardship, sacrifice, and finally death, **BUT HE HAD CHOSEN TO GO RATHER THAN TO STAY.**

There now arose a conflict in David Brainerd's life. Two great loves possessed him. There was the deep love for his sweetheart, Jerusha, and his love for God. At first he had hoped for a life of devotion and service together, but Brainerd was to discover a strange truth; he could not

Two great loves possessed him. There was the deep love for his sweetheart, Jerusha, and his love for God.

have both—*this side of heaven.* During his initial ministry among the Indians, Brainerd longed for Jerusha. In June at Crossweeksung, he felt he should settle down there as pastor, and this, of course, meant a fireside of his own with Jerusha. He wrote her a letter expressing this desire and love. A few days later as Brainerd contemplated the will of God for his life, he realized that he had made a mistake and that the love in his heart for Jerusha was clouding God's purpose for his life. Again he sat down to write, this time to say goodbye. He wrote a letter as tragic as any man ever wrote to his sweetheart: *"I love to be a pilgrim and a stranger in this wilderness…All my plans are broken off. I am constrained to say, 'Farewell…to the very dearest. Goodbye, I will spend my life to my last moment in caves and dens of the earth, if the Kingdom of Christ may thereby be advanced.'"*

This decision made by Brainerd on July 1, 1745, was in effect virtually "Suicide for Christ," as the consequences of it brought his life to a swift close. Brainerd's ministry among the Indians had been to this point fruitless and barren. He had not baptized a single convert. His health was failing, and he realized that it was a matter of time. However, tears were beginning to flow, and the Spirit of God was beginning to awaken the Indians to their need of salvation.

Brainerd was at the threshold of victory. It was now either ALL or NOTHING.

If he left the Indians now to settle down with Jerusha, all would be lost. Life with her in the wilderness would be impossible with such a pace. He made his decision to devote himself ruthlessly to the service of God with whatever life he had remaining.

For the next twenty-two months Brainerd poured out his blood and tears for the souls of the Indians. He doubled his efforts to reach the Indians. During the 31 months before this decision, he had ridden 7,500 miles preaching to the Indians. In just 16 months that followed, he rode another 7,500 miles doubling his efforts, and all this in early America with its stones, fallen logs, cold and snow, rain and mud, and in summer choking dust. Multitudes of the forgotten people were converted. One commented, "Him talk only of Jesus." Christ was the theme of the "Prophet of the Wilderness."

It was in the fall of 1746 that a lonely rider appeared on the horizon with the wilderness behind him, coming home to die. He coughed a great deal, and the furrows on his face told the story of hardship and distress. His body was now thin and his cheeks sunken. Once he was youthful and carefree. Now he was cautious and serious. Once his lips were full and relaxed. Now they were held in a firm line. Once a prince ready for the battle, now he was a soldier worn and weary. Death stared Brainerd in the face.

About May 1, he reached his hometown of Haddam and on May 28 he arrived in Northampton. A weary hand knocked on the door at the home of Jonathan Edwards…and of Jerusha. A few days later David and Jerusha rode over to Boston. This was June in England, and the beauty of spring adorned every mile.

Jerusha and David cherished the moments. The world was too beautiful for death, yet death was less than six weeks away. A few days later the couple returned the 90 miles back to Northampton. A few weeks later, Brainerd lay dying in the home of Jonathan Edwards. Gathering the Edwards' children and servants about him, he said, "I shall die here, and here I shall be buried, and you will see my grave. When you see my grave, remember what I said to you while I was alive; then think with yourself how the man who lies in that grave counseled and warned me to prepare for death."

Jonathan Edwards in this portion of his account wrote his summary of last times.

"David's last church service, the last time he prayed with the family, his last horseback ride, the last time he went out of our gates alive, his last messages," Edwards wrote, *"I praise God that in His providence Brainerd should die in my house so that I might hear his prayers, so that I might witness his consecration, and be inspired by his example."*

David Brainerd's last days were spent with the two great loves of his life, Jerusha and God. For hours they visited in silence, "her face close to his." Silent glances told all. Jonathan Edwards once said that David had remarked: "It's like a little piece of Heaven to have her near me."

One afternoon in early October, the dying man reached out and took Jerusha's hand. He wanted her to understand why he had decided not to marry her. Surely thoughts of what "might have been" filled their minds at this moment. What if she had been his wife? How lovely she was. Brainerd spoke, "Oh Jerusha! I could not have spent my life otherwise for the whole world." She understood and pressed his hand, tearfully putting her face close to his. Brainerd continued, "Jerusha, if I thought I should not see you and be happy with you in another world, I could not bear to part with you...But we shall spend a happy eternity together."

On Sunday, October 9, 1747, David Brainerd died and just four months later, Jerusha, too, passed through the valley to meet him. Edwards, recounting the death of his daughter, commented, "When she died, she whispered to him, 'Oh Father, I have desired nothing but to live for God and His glory...and David said to me he felt certain we would spend a happy eternity together.'" The broken-hearted father held back his tears, and added, "I'm sure David was right."

In an old churchyard at Northampton, Massachusetts, lies the grave of David Brainerd, and a few inches away the grave of Jerusha Edwards— together in death, but alive together forevermore in eternity. The two great loves of David Brainerd were now his to keep ...forever.

David Brainerd's Grave at Northampton
Beside him lies "Jerusha Edwards," his sweetheart.

Faith Promise

1851

Hudson Taylor, one of the poorest young preachers in England, learned a lesson that would make him rich for life.

The streets were pure gold. The street lamps glittered from their poles like brilliant diamonds sparkling in the night. The pavement stones echoed the tune of hymns as the rich, young prince made his way step by step back home.

The rich young prince was none other than Hudson Taylor, one of the poorest young preachers in England. The streets were the dismal and dreary pathways of a 19th century English city. But the preacher FELT rich and the streets SEEMED like gold because this night had become a monument of faith in his career for God. The events of this night would encourage him and preach to him all the days of his life.

A few hours earlier, Hudson Taylor, now nineteen years old, had been engaged in Gospel work in the lowest part of town. It was about 10 p.m. when Taylor was accosted by an Irishman who pleaded for him to come to his home to pray for his wife who was near death. The man, a Catholic, explained that he had asked the priest to come but his request was refused due to his inability to pay the priest a sum of money. The man explained that not only could he not pay the priest, but his family was starving.

The young preacher at once consented to go, but his thoughts went immediately to the one silver coin he possessed in his pocket. He, himself, had not been paid for days by his employer and he was nearing the end of his resources. His future meals consisted of two bowls of porridge in his apartment and the silver coin in his pocket.

He would eat one bowl before retiring to bed and the other upon rising for breakfast.

The silver coin would be his supply for the other meals. As the desperate man led him through the dismal streets of the city, the young preacher reached in his pocket and fingered his only coin to make sure that it was secure.

If he lost that coin, his own state would be desperate. Hudson became nervous as the two entered a court in the heart of the lower section of the city. Hudson had been there before witnessing for Christ. Besides being rough and poverty stricken, the area was strictly catholic.

On his previous visit to this court, he had been abused and his gospel literature torn up in his face. He was warned never to set foot in this court again or else. Now, late at night, he was being led by an unknown individual to this very place. Perhaps it was a trap. Perhaps the local thugs were lying in wait to "do him in."

Fearfully, he mounted a miserable flight of stairs, being led by his companion. The two reached the top of the stairs, and as the man fumbled with the door, Hudson must have wondered what he would face on the other side. Perhaps the thugs were there waiting and ready for him. The door opened and his fears were relieved.

There met his eyes five little children scattered about the room. Their eyes and sunken cheeks told the story of slow starvation. Turning his head around the room, his eyes now fastened upon a mother, weak and exhausted, lying sick and motionless on a ragged pallet. Taylor thought, "Ah, if I had two shillings and a sixpence instead of half a crown, how gladly would I give them one-and-sixpence of it." The young preacher tried to tell the group now before him that they could trust God, that they had a heavenly Father who would meet their needs if they would trust Him. His words stuck like balls of cotton in his throat. All he could see before him were hungry eyes and needs and then his one and only silver coin in his pocket. God seemed to say to him, "You hypocrite, telling these unconverted people about a kind and loving Father in Heaven and not prepared yourself to trust Him without half a crown." He thought, "If only I had two coins I would gladly give them one."

Finding it impossible to speak peace to the desolate people before him, Hudson decided to pray. Prayer was always a joy to him and he never seemed to lack for words. He felt that prayer would ease the situation and he could then go on his way,

By faith he had been led of God to GIVE ALL that he had, trusting God wholly to supply his own needs.

leaving the family at peace. The young preacher knelt and commenced to pray, "Our Father…"

Again he choked. God seemed to say, "Dare you call me Father and mock me…with this family before you and money in your pocket." Again he thought, "If the silver coin were divided

into smaller coins, I would even part with half of them. According to Taylor in later life, he experienced a moment of conflict unparalleled to any other in his life, before or after. Somehow he stumbled through a meaningless form of prayer and arose greatly distressed.

As he arose, the desperate father turned to him and said, "If you can help us, for God's sake, do." At that moment a verse from the Bible flashed in Hudson's mind, "Give to Him that asketh of thee." God had struck the final blow to his lack of faith. A hand reached into a pocket and fingers fastened around a silver coin. Pulling it out, he handed it over to the grateful father. Joy filled the young preacher's soul. Words came with ease and he felt every sentence.

Turning to the family, he said, "This is the last money I have on earth, but God is my Father and He can be trusted." As the young preacher left the slum-dwellers that night, he felt that not only had he helped save a woman's life, but he saved his own. By faith he had been led of God to GIVE ALL that he had, trusting God wholly to supply his own needs.

As he made his way through the streets, he sang at the top of his voice. He had no idea where his supply would come from after his last meal at breakfast, but although he had no food, he had God. That night as he sat down at his table to eat his next-to-the-last meal, he would not have exchanged it for the king's table.

It was like a feast. Sitting there eating his meager rations, a verse occurred to him, "He that giveth to the poor lendeth to the Lord." When he knelt to pray that night, he reminded God of His promise and asked that God repay him as soon as possible or he would go hungry the next day.

Early the next morning the landlady knocked on his door. When he opened the door, she stood there with a package in her hands. The handwriting was strange or forged and the postmark was blurred. He could not tell who had sent it and from where it had been mailed. Opening the package, he found a pair of gloves. Picking up the gloves, a gold coin fell out of one.

Hudson shouted, "Praise the Lord!" He had by faith invested a silver coin in the work of God just 12 hours before and now had received a gold coin, or 400 percent interest. He never found out where the gold coin came from, but it mattered not. God had sent it in answer to his faith promise and He had sent it right on time.

From this day on he would by faith invest in this bank, a bank which would never go broke. Through the hard and trying years in far-off China, Hudson Taylor often thought back to this event in his life and was strengthened.

In the fifty years that followed, Hudson Taylor prayed his way from death's door, prayed agnostics to Christ, and prayed ships out of treacherous waters. Over 5 million dollars came in, without public or private solicitation of funds, in answer to his prayers for his needs and the work in China.

From this day on he would by faith invest in this bank, a bank which would never go broke.

He prayed and over 900 young people answered the call of God for China. On the last day of his life, although he did not know it was the last, in a distant Chinese city, Hudson Taylor counseled a young man on the need of living by faith in God. His last words before going to bed… and to heaven were these: **"We can trust God fully."**

On one occasion Hudson Taylor spoke to a group of missionaries in China. One of those in the meeting jotted down his feelings and impressions:

"Mr. Taylor's subject was Phil. 3: that what we give up for Christ we gain, and what we keep back is our real loss. We seemed to lose sight of the speaker and to hear only the voice of the Holy Spirit. It was a time of humbling and confession, nearly every one was broken down…I cannot tell you what it was to sit there and hear Mr. Taylor tell of the hundreds of towns and cities he had passed, and not a single Christian in any of them! Vividly he described all this and the condition of the people: and there were we, comfortable and settled down, taking for granted perhaps that we had obeyed our Master's command, practically forgetting that Han-chung-fu was part of the world, and that people even in the villages at hand might never hear of Christ unless we set ourselves to go to them. The way in which he spoke of eternity—Life eternal or DEATH eternal—must have moved the coldest heart."

The Exploits of a Dead Man

"You are a dead man!" the doctor exclaimed. "Get home as fast as you can and arrange your affairs immediately." Piercing words were these for a man who wanted to go to China as a missionary.

The physician, a confirmed skeptic, offered Hudson Taylor no hope. Like a sentence of doom he provoked conflicting emotions in the young man's mind. "Why would God call me to China if I were to die in London?"

In preparation for China, Hudson Taylor was studying medicine in London. One day he pricked his finger with a needle while dissecting the body of a person who had died of a malignant fever. The tiny wound became infected during the autopsy, and he now had in his body the symptoms of death.

Upon receiving the fateful diagnosis, his first thought was one of sorrow that he could not go to China. Then, like a flash, Taylor thought, "I cannot die, for God has called me to China." Faith surged through his heart, and with emotions of sheer trust in the will of God, he turned to the doctor: "If I should die, I will have the joy of being with my Master in Heaven, but I believe that I shall not die. God has a work for me to do in China, and however severe the struggle, I must be brought through."

The doctor replied, "That is all very well, but you must go home at once. You have no time to lose; if you delay, you will soon be incapable of winding up your affairs." Hudson barely made it to his house where, after climbing three flights of stairs, he fainted. His uncle, finding him, called the doctor and cared for his needs.

After days of suffering, Hudson slowly recovered. God had seen him through. Still he learned that two other medical students who had been infected as he had died of the fever in another London hospital. He thanked the doctor for his kind attention and then told him of God's provision and care for him. The doctor listened intently as Hudson described how God had brought him from death's door, provided his needs, and answered his prayers. He was awed at the reality of God in this young man's life. Tears welled up in his eyes. Broken, he said, "I would give all the world for a faith like yours."

Hudson explained to the doctor that it could be his without money or price. The two never met again. When Hudson returned to London after a rest in the country, he learned that the doctor had suffered a stroke from which he never recovered. The doctor who attended this "dead man" was actually nearer death himself than was his patient. It was indeed true what the doctor had said: Taylor was a dead man—*dead to self* and alive in Christ. Accosted by death in London, he had been spared while the doctor to whom he witnessed was now dead. During his experience as a missionary, this "dead man" would often deal with death.

The "Dead Man's" Voyage

On September 19, 1853, the *Dumbries* sailed for China. The voyage had a rough beginning. Having barely left port, the vessel was caught in a violent storm, tossed to and fro in the Irish Channel for twelve days. At last on the open sea, Hudson found the voyage to be extremely tedious. Many days the ship, which depended wholly upon the wind, simply floated calmly along, making no progress, sometimes drifting backwards. On one occasion the ship, caught in a strong current, began drifting towards treacherous underwater reefs.

The crew in lifeboats tried desperately to turn the ship's direction, but all in vain. The Christian Captain said to Taylor, "We have done all we can." Taylor replied, "No, there is one thing we have not done yet. We have not prayed." Following a season of prayer, Hudson approached the first officer, a godless man, and asked him to set the sails. He looked at the dead calm and scorned the young missionary.

Taylor continued, "We have been asking a wind from God, and it is coming immediately. We are almost on the reefs and there is not a minute to lose." Again the first officer mocked, but while he was speaking, Taylor watched his eye, and followed it up to the royal (the topmost sail), and there, sure enough, the corner of the sail was beginning to tremble in the coming breeze. In a matter of minutes

It was indeed true what the doctor had said: Taylor was a dead man—dead to self and alive in Christ.

the ship veered away from the rocks to safety. Again death retreated from this "dead man," God's missionary to China.

The "Dead Man's" Vision

When Taylor was called to China, that country was closed to most foreigners and missionaries. As the *Dumbries* sailed into the yellow waters of a Chinese river on March 1, 1854, it was still quite an event for an Englishman, and especially a missionary, to appear in Shanghai unannounced.

After months of language study, Hudson found himself working full-time, teaching the Chinese population. His ministry proved more effective when he began dressing in Chinese clothing, although this brought some criticism from fellow workers. While traveling hundreds of miles inland and along the coast, his life was often in danger. Many times he was roughly treated and threatened by death. He suffered once at

the hands of robbers and had to pray his way back to his city of residence.

No matter what the test, his faith in God always prevailed. When the missions' committee in London went into debt to finance its missionary enterprises, Taylor resigned. It was his conviction that God was able to supply, and he took the Word "Owe no man anything" literally. Following the winning of his first convert, he joyfully wrote to his mother, "This morning my heart was gladdened by the request of Kue-hua to be baptized. I cannot tell you the joy this has brought me…if one soul is worth worlds, Mother, am I not abundantly repaid? And are not you too?"

Having lived for the salvation of souls in England, now, after weary months of language preparation, he was winning the souls of China. One outstanding convert was a businessman by the name of Mr. Nyi, who passed the open doors of the mission house one evening just at service time. A bell was ringing, announcing the service, and along with a number of other people, Mr. Nyi entered the door. He had heard that this "Jesus Hall" was a place where foreigners taught religion, and, being a devout Buddhist, he was interested.

As a Buddhist he too believed in life after death. Intently, he listened as the young foreigner in Chinese dress preached of the serpent lifted up in the wilderness, representing the Son of the God in Heaven. As Nyi sat listening to the Gospel, he felt a strange moving in his heart. Old things passed away, and Nyi became a new creature in Christ Jesus before the service was ended. As the service drew to a close and the missionary ceased to speak, Nyi stood to his feet, a new man

On the sandy beach at Brighton, England, Hudson Taylor committed to God the fate of the lost souls in China. He surrendered himself to God and established the China Inland Mission.

in Christ Jesus, and addressed the crowd. He said:

"I have long sought the Truth, as did my father before me, but without finding it. I have traveled far and near, but have never searched it out. In Confucianism, Buddhism, Taoism, I have found no rest; but I do find rest in what we have heard tonight. Henceforth, I am a believer in Jesus."

Nyi's profession of faith in Christ had great influence, as he was well known and respected. Sometime later, talking with Hudson Taylor, Nyi raised a question. "How long have you had the Glad Tidings in England?" he asked unsuspectingly. Hudson Taylor, a bit embarrassed, vaguely replied that England had possessed the Gospel for

several hundred years. A look of astonishment came upon the face of Nyi. "What," he exclaimed. "Is it possible that you have known about Jesus so long, and only now have come to tell us? My father sought the truth for more than twenty years and died without finding it. Oh, why did you not come sooner?"

On another occasion Taylor made a trip to the city of Shanghai by riverboat on a preaching tour. Among the passengers he found a Chinese man by the name of Peter who had been to England. He was an intelligent man who had heard something of the Gospel but had not accepted Christ. As Taylor told him of the reality of Christ, the man listened with attention and was moved to tears. He asked Taylor if he might accompany him the next day and hear him preach.

Later, as Taylor was in his cabin preparing literature for distribution, he heard a splash and a loud cry. Running to the deck, he saw that Peter was gone, with the crowd looking at the spot in the water where he had disappeared but making no effort to save him. A strong wind was carrying the junk rapidly forward. Hudson Taylor leaped overboard in hope of finding him. In the water, Hudson saw a nearby fishing boat with a peculiar dragnet which he knew could immediately bring up the drowning man.

He cried out, "Come drag here, a man is drowning." They replied, "Veh bin." *(It is not convenient...we are busy fishing.)* They bickered over money, and finally, when Hudson offered them all he had, they came and brought up the body with their net. Even while Hudson tried resuscitation to revive the dead man, they clamored to be paid. All was in vain.

Hudson Taylor remembered this incident throughout the years and paralleled it with the apathy in the West toward souls in distant lands. The fishermen were actually guilty of this Chinaman's death, for they had the means of saving him at hand if they would but have used them.

The "Dead Man's" Victory

Taylor made various return trips to England and even to America. God was leading him to establish a mission that would penetrate the interior. China was a treacherous land, however, and should he do it, it could mean martyrdom and suffering; and would not he be responsible? The feeling of bloodguiltiness became more and more intense. Because he did not ask for laborers, they did not come forward to go out to China, and every day tens of thousands were passing away to Christless graves.

Describing this emotion in his autobiography, he wrote: *"Perishing China so filled my heart and mind that there was no rest by day, and little sleep by night, till health broke down."* At the invitation of a friend, Hudson spent a few days in Brighton on the south coast of England. Walking along the sandy beach, he settled it all. He wrote:

"On Sunday, June 25, 1865, unable to bear the sight of a congregation of a thousand or more Christian people rejoicing in their own security, while millions were perishing for lack of knowledge, I wandered out on the sands alone, in great spiritual agony; and there the Lord conquered my unbelief, and I surrendered myself to God for this service."

Taylor committed the matter to God. The harvest was God's after all. At first, he asked for 24 workers, 2 for each of 11 inland provinces which were without a missionary, and 2 for Mongolia. God gave Hudson the 24, and many more followed. In 1865, the China Inland Mission was organized.

Forty years after that day on Brighton Beach when he decided to establish China Inland Mission, Taylor was sitting in a mission station in one of the far-off provinces of inland China. Now, over 800 missionaries were scattered over the whole vast interior of China. Although many had sealed their testimony by blood at various times, God's Word was going

Hudson Taylor died 50 years after the doctor gave him only a few days to live. In these 50 years, he established the China Inland Mission which grew in his lifetime to over 800 missionaries scattered over the whole vast interior of China.

out to the perishing multitudes who had never once heard.

As he looked out his window, Taylor might have thought of the truth of his statement uttered years before: *"God's work done in God's way will never lack God's supply."* The "dead man" had seen millions of dollars come for the work, with thousands and thousands of converts baptized. The next day the message spread: Hudson Taylor was dead; his work was ended.

This was not the first time Hudson had been pronounced dead. The first time was in the London hospital as a young man. "Go home, settle your affairs, you have no time to lose." And he seldom lost a moment in the service of Christ in China; for 50 years the "dead man" seldom lost a moment.

A Chinese evangelist leaned over his body that day and paid a fitting tribute. "Venerable Pastor," he said, holding one of Taylor's wrinkled hands in his two warm ones, "we have come to see you today. We are your little children, Venerable Pastor; you opened for us the road to Heaven; you loved us and prayed for us long years…

We love you."

A hand written concordance of the Bible

The Others

Doctor's Corner" - In secret she listened to Transworld Radio and gave mission reports to secret meetings of Christians.

James Ray examines a hand-cranked printing press used by the underground church.

Unknown!

**And others had trial
of cruel mockings...of
bonds and imprisonment:
They were stoned...were
slain with the sword...
(Of whom the world
was not worthy)**

–Hebrews 11:36-38

A collection of various items that were connected with the underground church in former communist Latvia was assembled for an exhibition. The items had been gathered from those Christians, most still alive, who had suffered imprisonment, beatings and persecution by the communist in that country. Others had paid with their lives and blood. This exhibition in Riga, Latvia, was a single moment in history. It was temporary. In a few days all the items in this room would be returned to individual owners and possibly would never be assembled together again as an exhibition. These rooms presented an awesome atmosphere of persecution and suffering–but MORE. Here in case after case lay a story of love and devotion to Jesus Christ–rare to Western ears and minds.

Asimple towel lay folded with a picture of a little girl placed on top. The towel, placed on the base of the doorway leading downstairs, was the signal that business in that room was underway. Looking down again at the picture, she said, "That little girl stood watch for those secret makers of the Bible–**I was that little girl!**"

Ilva's eyes fell upon the name of a hero "Charles H. Spurgeon." One of his whole books had been beautifully printed by hand. Spurgeon's book lay on top of scores of other hand printed religious books. These books represented thousands of hours of intense labor in dark, secret rooms.

Ilva's eyes moistened with deep emotion as she relayed to me her story of standing watch at the doorway to the room where Bibles were being copied.

"In this house," Ilva said, pointing to a picture, "many people were discovered and arrested." She continued, "There were no Bibles, no Bible-study books–no choruses. All such materials were illegal."

Her eyes moistened again; her voice took on a tone so completely in earnest that my own heart felt her emotion. "This is a picture of my grandmother. She handcopied 150 books."

"...and OTHERS...."

There was Marija Gorska. Her hands were almost paralyzed from disease. She bound up her fingers with cellophane tape to hold them steady and on a primitive typewriter pecked out 56 books. She recently died in 1995.

Various printing devices, mostly homemade, were gathered in the center of the room. There was the homemade mimeograph machine, the homemade bookbinder, the manual printing press and...oh yes...the copy machine with its windowpane glass. The glass pane was rounded and thick. The man who saw it located in a residential window gave every valuable thing he had on him in exchange for that windowpane. He then made a wooden box, situated the glass on top and placed a powerful light underneath. With special paper they could then print copies of music with the process.

"...and OTHERS...."

There was the doctor's corner. Her chair, table, phone, tape recorder and radio were repositioned just as it had been in her home not so many months ago when the communists were in power.

She was a well-trained surgeon noted for her success. The doctor, however, had a dark secret. At this desk she listened to Transworld Radio beamed out of Monte Carlo. She would tape the mission broadcasts and then type notes. The notes were compiled into a special report of missionary work in

Looking again at the hundreds of hand printed and typewritten books, I thought of my library with hundreds of references at my fingertip.

various countries around the world. These reports were secretly circulated hand to hand among Christians in Latvia. They would be read in secret meetings.

I was amazed that in this dark, persecuted corner of Europe, Christians were rejoicing in the work of missionaries around the world. I tried to push out the thoughts of prayer letter boards in churches in the West and the flood of church members passing them without even a glance.

The doctor's secret was discovered. She was dismissed from her position and deprived of her large apartment.

She still rejoiced. This was the Lord's way of saving her the expense of large utilities. "The apartment was too large–anyway."

"…and OTHERS…."

Ilva told again of her special ministry of guarding the door–hiding those workers below. Along with the famine of Bibles was a scarcity of music and choruses. The workers in the room below carefully cut printed words from secular volumes to be pasted, letter by letter, onto a sheet of paper creating Gospel choruses.

In those last moments with Ilva, my own world flashed before me. Looking again at the hundreds of hand printed and typewritten books, I thought of my library with hundreds of references at my fingertip.

Those who had so LITTLE had given so MUCH…and I who had so much had given so little. I felt small. I had at first felt gratitude for the freedom of my world but now I witnessed a world without all the flair–a world of Christians who were GIANTS in the Kingdom of God–"…the OTHERS…."

I had read of the persecution in Hebrews 11, chronicling the accounts of Noah, Moses and Abraham and finally "…the Others…." God had allowed me to MEET some of the "others."

I left Ilva and her collection of memories with a feeling of awe unlike anything I have ever felt. **I knew for a few moments of my life I had been with "them" through the darkness.**

I had glimpsed the light in the dungeon and the fellowship of HIS SUFFERING….

The home of E.M. Bounds

still stands in the center of

Washington, Georgia, as a

memorial to its owner, a

prayer giant and the author

*of **Power through Prayer.***

E.M. Bounds

E.M.Bounds
THE PROPHET OF PRAYER

The stately old mansion in Washington, Georgia, now utilized as the Washington-Wilks Museum, is an architectural masterpiece of an era. Often driving through the town, the author noticed the house with only a faint interest in the architecture of an era long gone.

Some time later when he held meetings in the city, he was informed that the old museum was once the home of E.M. Bounds —the famous writer on the subject of prayer. The beautiful old mansion at once assumed new meaning.

Visiting the home of Bounds was like visiting the cave of Elijah where he talked with God. The emotion of the place took on the atmosphere of the upper room of Elisha when he met God in the time of the widow's crisis. Here E.M. Bounds met God in the early hours of the morning, pleading for sinners.

Edward McKendree Bounds was born in 1835. Lyle Wesley Dorsett in his book describes the early life of the family.[1] "Thomas Jefferson Bounds married Hester A. Purnell in 1823. Both were 22 years old.

The family had settled in Kentucky by 1827 and later moved to Mississippi where land was fertile and less expensive. Edward's father died in 1849 at the age of 49. Edward was only 14 at the time. Edward Bounds attended school in a one room school house. On June 9, 1854, at age 19, he passed the bar and was licensed to practice as an attorney-at-law in Missouri."

Although Edward Bounds had become a successful lawyer, he continued his search for meaning and purpose. By 1859, he had made a personal decision for Christ. Reading the biographies of great men, such as John Wesley, John Fletcher and David Brainerd, created a desire to do more in life than merely live. Before the end of 1859, he was preaching in a small Methodist Church and in 1860 was officially licensed to preach by the Methodist Conference.

The Soldier

When the Civil War erupted, his home state of Missouri was divided. Two of the Bounds' brothers joined the Union Army. Edward's sympathies were with the Confederacy. He became a chaplain in the Confederate military.

Earlier in February of 1861, Edward had assumed the pastorate of the Methodist Episcopal Church at Brunswick, Missouri. This church was located in pro-slavery Charitan County. The group of churches, of which this church was a part, had previously succeeded from the main body of Methodists over the issue of slavery.

As soon as Abraham Lincoln became President, federal troops occupied Missouri, confiscating church buildings, schools and all properties of the pro-slavery Methodist Church South. Federal troops met Bounds at his redbrick church in Brunswick and announced that he was under arrest. He was imprisoned in a federal prison in St. Louis, Missouri, until 1863 when he was freed in a prisoner exchange at Memphis, Tennessee.

That same year Bounds was sworn in as a regular chaplain for the Third Missouri Volunteers Infantry Regiment. As a chaplain, Bounds showed great courage. Dorsett in his work describes his ministry as a chaplain.[2]

"Chaplain Bounds may have been little in stature, but he was not short on courage. To be sure, he ministered in the hospitals and led prayer meetings, and worship in camp, but he traveled on foot with the army. He never dodged the front line of battle. He won the deep respect of his men because he loved them, marched with them, and never flinched from the heat of battle."

In the Battle of Franklin, Tennessee, many of Bound's men in his Missouri Infantry

Visiting the home of Bounds was like visiting the cave of Elijah where he talked with God.

were slaughtered. In 1865, he returned to Franklin and with a group of local men exhumed the bodies, identified them by name and gave them a proper burial on the Carter Farm where they had fallen.

In his wallet he placed a list of the soldiers he buried at Franklin. Many of these men he knew personally, having been their chaplain. On a personal basis, he had prayed with them and encouraged them toward Christ.

The Pastor

After the war ended in 1866, Bounds not yet 30 years old became pastor at a discouraged Methodist Church in Franklin, Tennessee. The two years he served at Franklin lifted the church from a depressed state to a state of revival. Bounds contributed the change to prayer. Gathering a group of men around him, Bounds prayed for over a year for revival.

Suddenly revival fell upon the struggling little congregation. Over 150 people were converted. This was Edward Bounds' first real test of the power of prayer. One of the converts of Bounds' revival ministry at Franklin was the renowned B. F. Haynes, who later became the third president of Asbury College. Haynes speaking of Bounds' influence wrote:

"When I was only a lad there came to Franklin, Tennessee, where we lived, as pastor of our church, the Reverend E. M. Bounds. His preaching and life did more to mould and settle my character and experience than any pastor I ever had. His preaching profoundly impressed me, his prayers linger until today, as one of the holiest and sweetest memories of my life."

Bounds later pastored churches in St. Louis, Missouri, and Selma, Alabama, and for a number of years served as associate editor of the *Christian Advocate* (1890 -

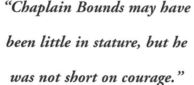

"Chaplain Bounds may have been little in stature, but he was not short on courage."

1894) in Nashville, Tennessee. Through his writing, Bounds encouraged Christians to rely on Scripture and to study the great lives of Brainerd, Louis Harms and others. He later resigned his position with the *Christian Advocate,* protesting the liberalism creeping into the Methodist Church. When the conference dismissed the famous Sam Jones, Bounds lined up with Jones in protest.

The remainder of his life was spent in the inherited mansion at Washington, Georgia, until his death in 1913. From this location, E.M. Bounds traveled on various preaching engagements, sometimes to the old Methodist campground at Indian Springs, Georgia.

This writer remembers attending meetings at Indian Springs as a young Christian. Indian Springs was a conclave of old Methodist Gospel preaching. Now reflecting, I can visualize Edward Bounds there. It was a perfect environment for his old-time fervent convictions.

When Bounds moved to Washington, Georgia, the population numbered only 3000 –much less than St. Louis or Nashville. The total population of the county was 18,000 (6,000 whites and 12,000 blacks). The town had a new public school, a railroad depot and several thriving businesses along with county offices. The town was smaller than Nashville but still pleasant and convenient.

The little city was a far cry from the limelight of St. Louis and the public exposure of the *Christian Advocate.* His ministry would never again be as public as during those days. When Bounds resigned his position with the *Christian Advocate*, he would pay this price.

The Prayer Giant

There at Washington, Bounds grew close to God. There he ventured into a deeper prayer life. Dorsett comments:

"Sometimes Bounds would lie flat on his back praying to God. But many hours were spent on his knees, or lying face down in a prone posture where he could be heard weeping for the conversion of sinners and sanctification of preachers." [3]

Usually Bounds was up at 4 am interceding with God for sinners. Towards the last part of his life, he arose at 3 am for prayer. Back in Missouri as a young lawyer, Bounds had interceded on behalf of men. Now in Washington, Georgia, nearing the end of his life, he interceded for men's souls before the Judge of the Universe. Between the event of a young lawyer and that of a devout servant of God, God had tempered his servant by trials.

As the author of this article walked through the old house in Washington, Georgia, he felt the spirit of long ago. He could imagine the sound of prayers echoing against the hard wooden walls. Almost he could visualize the old prophet of Washington kneeling and pouring out his soul to God.

The old preacher at Washington had a lot to remember. Memories surely surfaced again and again. His mind drifted back to Emmie, his first wife, who at 49 died, leaving him with 3 children. Perhaps his mind went back to that day in 1890 when news came to him of the death of his son

–six-year-old Edward. He had left the family in Georgia only a few weeks earlier to continue his work at Nashville.

Bounds had boarded a train to Georgia to gather with his family and to bury little Edward. He arrived in Washington on Thursday. The sorrow and tears mingled with the falling rain. The rain was so intense that the boy could not be buried until several days later.

One year later the sorrowful scene was repeated with the death of Charley, only eight days past his first birthday. Perhaps the bloody scenes of civil war and dying young men replayed. Sorrow and tears

"His preaching profoundly impressed me, his prayers linger until today, as one of the holiest and sweetest memories of my life." - B.F. Haynes

had tempered the prayers that echoed against the walls of the old mansion at Washington.

During this time Bounds wrote his book on heaven. In that book he wrote:

"We folded their hands with tears and kissed the lips and laid them to sleep. We wrote on their tombs the words of hope and resurrection. We did not see their spirits and could not follow them in their heavenward flight. Christ shall bring them back to us out of their graves and out of their sleep to our embrace and to our hearts."

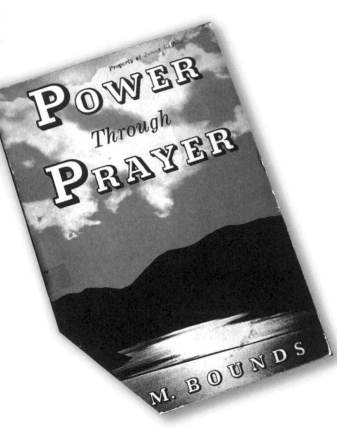

His most famous work was

Power Through Prayer.

Originally published in 1907,

the book is still in print.

Few books have influenced

so many people.

The Author

Billy Sunday read *Power Through Prayer* and was moved. Sunday also incorporated material from the book in some of his sermons.

When Bounds left the limelight to honor his convictions, others might have thought him foolish. Almost 100 years later, no one knows the editor of the *Christian Advocate* but the name of E.M. Bounds immediately brings our thoughts to prayer and to Christ.

Just nine days after he celebrated his 78th birthday, a white-haired gentleman in Washington, Georgia, closed his eyes and quietly slipped away. Dr. Edward McKendree Bounds joined the great heroes of the faith who had inspired him. Six months later his wife, only 56, followed him, and the old house in Washington fell silent. There would be no more the sound of footsteps of the prayer giant–no more the pleading voice to God at 4 am–and no more the weeping over souls.

The old mansion still stands in the center of town known only to the locals as the Washington-Wilks Historical Museum–but to us who know, it stands for E.M. Bounds–the MAN WHO TAUGHT US HOW TO PRAY.

[1] *E.M. Bounds, Man of Prayer,* Lyle Dorsett, Zonderson Publishing Company.

[2] Ibid.

[3] *E. M. Bounds* by Lyle Wesley Dorsett, page 54, Zondervan 1991.

I love Flowers

Rugged hands of this Russian lay pastor

in Ukraine held flowers for

"the great preacher from America"

—but I knew where the true greatness lay.

Flowers! I love them. I have seen the English country gardens throughout Great Britain with gorgeous colors of the rainbow. The great castles and manor houses of Europe, including Versailles, are adorned with unbelievable floral splendor. The tulip farms of Holland are nothing less than fields of glory.

I think, though, that the most beautiful bouquet of flowers I ever saw was deep in southern Ukraine.

Landing in Bucharest, we then traveled 13 hours over rugged Romanian roads. Darkness fell and the deep blackness of the night brought a foreboding emotion. Here and there a hay wagon and horses appeared out of the darkness, driven by a farmer and his wife. These ancient vehicles had no reflectors and were almost invisible until illuminated by our van lights. We felt terrified lest our driver not be able to stop the van in time.

For hours we waited at the Ukrainian-Romanian border while the communist guards followed their usual intimidation procedure. After crossing the border, we at last arrived at Chernivtsi in the Ukraine. A few hours later with a local pastor in his car, we headed out into the country. My assistant and I were to preach that day in three country churches. The car reeked with the smell of gasoline. The air was filled with choking dust mixed with fumes. We were absolutely fatigued. My body told me, "James, you can't do this any more. Let others do it. Stay in America. You have a nice office there."

We turned off the rugged main road and pointed the car down a one lane track. I wondered if anyone actually lived in such a seemingly remote area. Then I saw him…with *his bouquet of flowers,* standing alone alongside the trail…the pastor… waiting for us. His tall lanky frame looked like that of Abe Lincoln.

The day was planned with music, preaching and dinner on the grounds under the trees beside the little church in Ukraine.

He wore a suit, not quite fitting–without doubt–a lifetime investment. A closer glance revealed deep lines in his face mitigated by a look of gentleness. His rugged hands fastened around the bouquet of flowers which he had gathered earlier just for ME, the AMERICAN. It was probably true that Brant and I were the first Americans ever to come to this village, at least in a lifetime.

Pushing the flowers into my hands, he spoke words of welcome in Russian. I felt the honor of a king. These simple country folks had been under communism all of their lives. This visit of a preacher from America was for them a special event. This lay pastor had lived a life of toil and hardship. His existence had been a race for sheer survival.

In a country where preachers' tongues had been cut out of their mouths for preaching, he had never flinched. **He had held on through the darkness.**

To the Godly country people of the Ukraine, America had always been the symbol of freedom. During the years of persecution, bits and pieces of information handed down from generations were imbedded in their thinking about *America.* *America* was the greatest Christian nation on earth. The image, although faulty, existed. Any *preacher* from *America* would surely be holy and noble and Godly. Rugged hands held flowers for the "great preacher" from AMERICA–but I knew where the true greatness lay.

The day was planned with music, preaching and dinner on the grounds under the trees beside the little church. We laughed together, ate together and sang the praises of God, mixing the two languages. I remember it all– with great pleasure and sweetness–but beyond all the scenes that linger still in my memory, I shall forever remember…

"A BOUQUET OF FLOWERS."

"Should I be carried to the skies

On flowery beds of ease,

When others fought to win the prize,

And sailed through bloody seas."

The Loneliest Grave in
Scotland

Not long ago I drove out to Haddington near Edinburgh and visited the old Abbey Kirk. That day I stood at the grave of Jane Welsh Carlyle, the wife of Thomas Carlyle.

The inscription on her grave read:

"For 40 years, she was the true and loving helpmate of her husband and by act and word worthily forwarded him as none else could in all worthy he did or attempted. She died at London the 21st of April 1866, suddenly snatched from him, and the light of his life as if gone out."

As I stood there at Haddington that day, a feeling of intense loneliness swept over me. I thought of her story. When Thomas Carlyle died in 1881 at the age of 85 and biographers began pouring over his personal papers, a startling discovery was made.

The faithful, beautiful and gentle wife of the great writer had been often ignored, slighted and taken for granted. She had lived unappreciated for over 40 years while her husband lived for one thing–**HIMSELF** and his career as a writer.

Publicly Tom Carlyle was one of the most eminent of Victorian writers but privately he was moody, eccentric and self-centered. He was away in Scotland when Jane Welsh died in London. When he received the telegram with news of her death, HIS WORLD FELL APART.

"For 40 years she was the true and loving helpmate of her husband…SUDDENLY SNATCHED FROM HIM, and the light of his life…GONE OUT."

Carlyle returned to London. Walking through the streets of memory, he made his way to the place where he and Jane first met. Suddenly forty years of memories swept over his heart. How much he had taken for granted.

Now all of his writings became nothing. What he had treasured most was as but empty air. His true treasure had been Jane Welsh.

He lamented:

"I looked up at the window of the old room where I had first seen her–1821 on a Summer evening after sunset–five and forty years ago. She was the most beautiful creature I had ever beheld, sparkling with grace and talent…Oh to think of that now. The funeral was at one on Thursday. Only twelve old friends were there. I laid her in the grave…and ALL WAS ENDED. With the skies looking down on her, there sleeps my little Jeannie, and the light of her face will never shine on me more."

The faithful, beautiful and gentle wife of the great writer had been often ignored, slighted and taken for granted.

It has been said that the saddest sentence in English literature is that sentence written in his diary, *"Oh, that I had you yet for five minutes by my side, that I might tell you all."* I have never stood at a grave just like this one, surely the loneliest grave in Scotland. I suspect that there are many such graves scattered across this planet–graves of "too late" or "missed opportunity."

"Oh…if I could see her once more…for five minutes, to LET HER KNOW…" but he could never see her again. His heart was breaking. I have had people say to me, "If I could go back…if I could live my life over again…," but you can't go back. I can never forget a dear man in my home church, a deacon, who confided to me that God had called him to the mission field when he was a young man. He had neglected that call until it was too late. His heart was grieved. NOW is the time to obey God. NOW while you can. NOW while there is hope for earth's millions. NOW while you still have life. Soon it will be too late. It is not TOO LATE NOW to pray…to give…to go, to yield…to be what God wants you to be. **NOW** is the accepted time.

When the present becomes the past… it can never be undone.

The saddest words of tongue or pen… the saddest are these… IT MIGHT HAVE BEEN.

An American cemetery outside the city of Cambridge, England

Pass the Torch to Others

There is an American cemetery just outside the old university city of Cambridge, England. This plot of ground located in the deep, green countryside is a beautiful, immaculate place. The grounds are kept religiously, giving an impression of a Garden of Eden. It is a touching experience to go there.

The scene is highlighted by a long, reflecting pool bordered by a wall of names. At one end of the pool stands a towering monument in the form of a torch. At the opposite end of the pool there is erected a memorial hall.

Within the walls of this magnificent building there is to be found an engraved plaque dedicated to four American airmen. These airmen could have bailed out of their flaming plane but had they made that choice, their plane would have fallen on a nearby English Village. In a few seconds of time these four men made a life-sacrificing decision…to die…**so that OTHERS COULD LIVE.** The people of this village never forgot that act of sacrifice. By their placing this plaque of remembrance in the memorial hall, their children and generations to follow would be aware of four men who died for OTHERS.

The amazing story of sacrifice had just begun. Exiting the building, one sees the striking white wall bearing the names of 5,000 other American young men…who never made it home, whose bodies rested in that cemetery.

How often those young men must have thought of home…wanted home…longed to hug parents, brothers, sisters, wives. How many visions of mother's kitchen, the old home place and loved ones lay buried here.

The beautiful pool, extending the entire length of the wall, bore in its silent waters the reflection of 5,000 names…of men who died for OTHERS. Upon the great tower situated at the west end of the pool, a huge stone hand holds a flaming torch.

Engraved in stone are the words "TO YOU WITH FAILING HANDS WE PASS THIS TORCH. IT IS YOURS TO BE HELD HIGH." This spot was the most striking of all. Standing here, my gaze beheld the beautiful wall, the building of sacrifice, the pool of names, but more. In all directions from this point were rows and rows, hundreds of rows, of white crosses. What could one say to describe such a scene–such sacrifice? Only one word…OTHERS. They lived and died for OTHERS. Don't let the torch die–Pass it on to…

OTHERS.

JOHN AND BETTY STAM
WERE HERE!

Some years ago the author was invited to speak at the Madison Avenue Baptist Church of Patterson, New Jersey. This was the sending church of John and Betty Stam. The pastor, Dr. Clarence Sexton, had assumed the pastorate of the church when it had become discouraged and defeated by a changing neighborhood. In just a few months this man of vision had led the congregation back to its initial missionary zeal and fervor.

I considered it an honor to speak in a place where John and Betty Stam once sat and heard the challenge to missions. What a privilege to stand and speak where they stood and challenged their home church for China. The beautiful old building was refurbished to its original state. The pews were packed and the congregation listened to my challenge for missions. Perhaps, I thought, some young hearers…like John and Betty Stam…would catch the vision. Perhaps some young heart would surrender.

After all was said and done, however, the one most affected by being in such a place…was…I!

Helen Priscilla Stam was carried to Wuhu in a rice basket by Evangelist Lo. She was dressed in this outfit by her mother on the day that Mr. and Mrs. Stam were captured by Communists.

A Little Baby cries in China!

The crying of a little baby echoed against the walls of the deserted home in Miaosheo, China. Darkness had fallen upon the streets of the city. Even if the little baby's cries had penetrated walls and pierced the darkness of the night, no one would have dared to answer, for Miaosheo was in Communist hands, and many believers had already paid for their faith in blood. Out on the hillside overlooking the city, the little one's missionary mother and father lay silent and still, having sealed their testimony for Christ by death. A little baby cried in China, helpless and hopeless in an abandoned house, with no one to care, no one to hear…yet GOD, who sees even

the sparrow fall, hears and knows
and is in control.

A baby cried…in Albion, Michigan, just a handful of years before this dark and dismal day in Miaosheo. Dr. and Mrs. Ernest Scott were the proud parents of a baby girl they chose to call Betty. Soon afterward they became missionaries to China in the northern province of Shantung where Betty grew up. The Scott children could all testify in later years of parents who were loving, disciplined and of a home where Christ had the first place. One of the greatest influences in Betty's life was the example of her parents at

Out on the hillside

overlooking the city,

the little one's missionary

mother and father lay

silent and still, having

sealed their testimony for

Christ by death.

home. Betty, with her love of poetry, expressed her devotion to them in lines such as:

"Imagine, in God's certain Heaven,
Your children made forever glad,
praising the Lord for having given,
the dearest parents ever had."

All five of the Scott children expected at that time to return to China as missionaries. Although the parents had never suggested this to them, it was a spontaneous feeling that this was the natural thing to do. Soon after returning to the States, Betty was stricken with inflammatory rheumatism which left her heart so weakened that she was forced to lie flat on her back for months. During this time Betty drew close to God, often expressing her feeling in poetry. In the days following this event, Betty wrote to her parents, expressing God's moving hand in her life:

"I don't know what God has in store for me.
I am willing to be an old maid all my life,
if God wants me to. It's as clear as daylight
to me that the only worth-while life is one
of unconditional surrender to God's will."

Betty was now ready to do God's will whatever it was. She was HIS. Expressing the struggle and victory of this hour of her life, she penned

"I'm standing, Lord:
There is a mist that blinds my sight.
Steep, jagged rocks, front, left and right,
Lower, dim, gigantic, in the night.
Where is the way?

I'm standing, Lord:
The black rock hems me in behind,
Above my head a moaning wind, Chills an
oppressed head and mind. I am afraid.

I'm standing, Lord:
The rock is hard beneath my feet;I nearly
slipped, Lord, on the sleet. So weary, Lord,
and where a seat? Still must I stand?

I'm standing, Lord:
Since Thou hast spoken, Lord, I see Thou
hast beset these rocks are Thee. And since
Thy love encloses me, I stand and sing."

Betty had been a student at Moody Bible Institute for about a year when she noticed John Stam, a tall, attractive young man who, like herself, was destined to become a missionary to China. Betty, with her dark straight hair parted on one side, her soft and gentle disposition and high idealism towards the will of God, struck a chord in John's heart. John, too, had a godly home very similar to hers.

Also, he too had expressed a willingness to go to China alone and unmarried if God so willed. Both young people shared a common goal and love for China. Completing her education at Moody a year earlier than John, Betty became a missionary appointee to China. Her date of departure drew near. Walking by the lake in Chicago one day, they talked. It was apparent to both that they were in love. Their lives were meant to be blended into a beautiful oneness in the service of Christ.

Betty sailed for China. After finishing Moody, John was accepted for service as a missionary to China on July 1, 1932. A few months later John and Betty were married in China on the morning of

Both young people shared a common goal and love for China. Their lives were meant to be blended into a beautiful oneness in the service of Christ.

John and Betty Stam

October 25. It was a perfect day, not a cloud in the sky and without wind or dust. A tennis court was converted into an open-air chapel. Long benches with backs, brought over from the compound church, were arranged to leave a wide aisle down the center. Rugs covered the cement floor down the center aisle. Reuben A. Torrey, the son of Dr. R. A. Torrey, conducted the ceremony. The bridesmaids, wearing lavender silk and carrying bouquets of yellow chrysanthemums and asparagus fern tied with wide yellow ribbons, came slowly down the central aisle, followed by the maid of honor. The beautiful bride, on the arm of her father, came down the aisle, her eyes transfixed on the face of her bridegroom waiting at the altar. John's countenance beamed as he looked upon her.

Following the wedding, John and Betty left for Tsingtao, the home of her childhood. It was a beautiful honeymoon. In the months that followed, John and Betty completed their language study and entered heart and soul into the Chinese work. On one survey trip (into the region where they later died), they encountered a man, a school teacher, who had at one time bought a Gospel bound up with Acts from a colporteur passing through that region. The school teacher had spent many hours reading and searching the book and had become convinced that it was the Word of God. When the colporteur returned, the school teacher asked him if there were not more of this story.

Reading the Gospels and Acts had convinced him that it was only a part of a larger book. The colporteur had then secured the rest of the Book and so here was a man who possessed the entire Bible, whose testimony had led others to Christ.

John and Betty never lost their desire for the salvation of souls.

The surveys were over rugged and dangerous terrain, but John and Betty delighted in this, the will of God for their lives. On September 11, 1934, Betty gave birth to their daughter, Helen Priscilla. Communists were beginning to make inroads into certain districts throughout China. Being assured of safety in his district by the magistrate of Miaosheo, John and Betty arrived near the end of November with their few belongings and set up their home in a large old Chinese house. They never lost their desire for the salvation of souls. Later, on a piece of trampled paper in that home in Tsingteh that had been so happy, someone found a poem written by Betty Stam, which expressed her desire for souls. It partly read:

"Open my eyes, that I may see
this one and that one needing Thee,
Hearts that are dumb, unsatisfied,
Lives that are dead, for whom Christ died.
Someone to bring, dear Lord to Thee;
Use me, 0 Lord, use even me."

The last day of their home life together was December 5. A sudden attack, and the Red forces captured the city. Betty was bathing the baby when the warning came. Before they could escape, the Communists were at the door, demanding money and goods. Betty prepared tea and cakes for them, but nothing impressed the ruthless mad men. Taking John to the Communist headquarters, they soon returned for Betty and the baby. A few hours later, John managed to write the following letter amidst the turmoil and destruction:

"Dear Brethren: My wife, baby and myself are today in the hands of the Communists…the Lord bless and guide you, and as for us, may God be glorified, whether by **life or by death.***"*

The Communists decided to kill little Helen to torment the parents. When a Chinese believer pleaded for mercy for the child, the captors sneered, "Then it's your life for hers!" The old farmer replied, "I am willing." He was slain on the spot.

The last sacred hours, John and Betty were confined in a room of an abandoned rich man's home, with John being tied to the bedpost. Every glance and every word between John and Betty were now priceless and sacred. The Communists came and led them out to die. Later reports told of the calmness and peace in John and Betty's faces as they were led through the streets and ridiculed by the Communists.

Led to a little hill outside the city, they were commanded to kneel. A doctor who tried to intercede was taken away and slain. A flash of the sword and John and Betty Stam sealed their testimony with their own blood. Little Helen Priscilla was left abandoned in a house to die. It is a miraculous story within itself of how she was smuggled out of China to safety, proving that God was in control.

One might ask what it is that strangely draws a man or woman to a foreign and heathen culture, to people who will resent and despise them for being aliens, who will persecute and even kill them in the end? What is it that compels a man to love and endure all for such people? It is the love of Christ. The God-hating Communists must have reveled in the death of the Stams, priding themselves in ending their work. Little could they know that their murder of these two

Helen Priscilla Stam

would prompt seven hundred students at Moody Bible Institute to surrender to take their place. Two valiant soldiers lay dead on a Chinese hillside, a little baby cried alone in an abandoned house. But far from ending a movement, the Communists had planted the seed of a mighty harvest.

"Except a corn of wheat fall into the ground and die, it abideth alone; but if it die, it bringeth forth much fruit."

Grave of Reuben Archer Torrey at Montrose

Reuben Torrey

The Grave At Montrose

The times were trying and America and the world needed something to believe in. Torrey gave them something to believe in, and that something was—God!

On a hill overlooking Montrose, Pennsylvania, the author stood for a moment of reflection. Just in front of his feet was the grave of R. A. Torrey. Reuben Torrey died on October 26, 1928, in Asheville, North Carolina. Longtime friend Rev. Will Houghton, pastor of the Atlanta Baptist Tabernacle, conducted the service. He had accompanied Reuben's body on the train from Asheville to Montrose. His final resting place belonged at Montrose.

Etched in the granite stone were the words:

Reuben Archer Torrey
1856 - 1928
"I have fought a good fight,
I have finished my course,
I have kept the faith."

Just a few yards down the hill along the path were the tabernacle and campground where Torrey organized great meetings. Those meetings changed the lives of thousands.

In the tabernacle, the old pulpit over which the powerful, moving, convicting voice thundered forth the message of God now stood silent and dusty. Still farther along the same road, situated near the center of town, was the beautiful old Victorian house–the home of R. A. Torrey.

Reuben Archer Torrey was born in Hoboken, New Jersey, just a few years before the nation was plunged into a bloody civil war. He died at Asheville, North Carolina, October 26, 1928. His life spanned a time of civil war– through the healing of a broken nation to the World War I and almost to World War II.

The times were trying and America and the world needed hope and a Word from God. Life was hard and men needed something to believe in. Torrey gave them something to believe in, and that something was–GOD!

The world *almost* missed him. *Almost* the hundreds of thousands did not hear. *Almost* all the mighty blessings to be

poured forth remain in the vessel of mercy. *"Almost"* hinged on one night and one event and one decision. That one event occurred on a night in 1869 in a small room. Reuben Torrey came to a crossroad. His decision at that crossing would mean *life or death*.

Awaking from a dream in which his mother asked him to preach, Reuben sat up in bed. It seemed so real! Depression seized his mind and emotions. *He* could never preach.

His godless life convicted him. His mother's prayers were pulling him toward God while his worldly life that he loved, like a weight,

Reuben Torrey

was pulling him down. Torrey's father was a lawyer and banker before losing everything in a financial reversal. His mother, Elizabeth, was a dedicated and refined Christian woman.

Her prayers and concern for Reuben had not been a secret. One day he said to her, "I don't want to hear about my sins and your prayers; I'm going to Yale and will not bother you any more." With tear-filled eyes, Elizabeth followed him to the gate.

His mind was made up. He would decide for himself about life. With a heavy heart, Torrey's mother planted one more witness in Reuben's mind: "Son, when you come to the end of your rope and everything seems hopeless, call upon God with all your heart and He will surely help you!"

The great success of the Moody Bible Insitute owes much, if not all, of the credit to Ruben Torrey.

Desiring to become a lawyer as his father, Reuben entered Yale University. There he increased greatly the distance between his Christian training and the world. The evils of the day attracted him. The pull was too strong to resist and besides…he thought, "I am happy. These are the things I love." What Reuben had not counted on were the problems that came with it all… problems he could not deal with alone. He described his vain search for happiness: "I found disappointment; I found despair; I found utter wretchedness and barrenness."

The lights of the dance, the card games, the race track faded that

night in 1869 when he awoke from his disturbing dream. In utter remorse and despair he seized on the thought of ending his life. He would use a razor to kill himself, but the razor had vanished. Where was it? In vain he searched the room for something–*anything* –with which to cut himself but found *NOTHING.*

Now the words of his mother replayed. He could still hear her pleading at the gate, "When you come to the end of your rope and *everything seems hopeless,* call upon God with all your heart and He will help you!"

Reuben Archer Torrey

J. Kennedy MaClean writes about this incident: "He did not know at the time, but he afterwards learned, that at the very moment when life seemed so black and hopeless, and when he contemplated ending it, his mother, over four hundred miles away, was on her knees before God, beseeching Him to save her son."[1] Falling on his knees he prayed, *"O God, if there is such a Being, I need Your help. If You will give it to me, I'll follow You…I'll even preach."* In that moment of decision, a peace swept Reuben that remained with him until his dying day.

An audience of 7,000 people at Bolton

So much hinged on the lonely night at Yale. The eternal destiny of thousands waited in the vacuum of moments. Had Reuben Torrey taken the other road that night, there would have been no grave at Montrose– only a mound of dirt in another state covering a young boy–a SUICIDE!

Torrey immediately made his faith known at Yale. Following his experience at Yale, the young man became an ardent soul winner.

After training for the ministry, he was ordained in 1878, and in 1879 married Clara Smith, a fervent Christian woman. Clara lies beside him on the hill at Montrose.

In 1878, he became pastor of a church at Garretsville, Ohio, a small village with a population of 1000. Later in 1887, he spent time at the People's Church.[2] Everything Torrey did, he did well. He was a born organizer and an ardent scholar. He possessed an unusual ability to "put things together" and make them work.

Eventually when D. L. Moody needed someone to lead his new institute at Chicago (now Moody Bible Institute), Torrey was recommended and accepted. The great success of the Bible institute, especially in its initial stages, owes much, if not all, credit to Rueben Torrey. He led the institute from its beginning on September 26, 1889, until the year 1908.

He accepted the call to the Chicago Avenue Church (later Moody Church) as well as leading the institute. D. L. Moody was delighted that Torrey accepted the church. Roger Martin, in his excellent work on Torrey, describes the blessings upon the ministry at Moody Church: "When he accepted the pastorate, the church building would seat 2,200 people

–1,200 on the main floor and 1000 in the gallery. In the preceding years, the gallery had been opened only on special occasions or when Mr. Moody was there. Almost immediately it became necessary to open the gallery. And in the evening service, with every inch of standing room taken, as many as 2,700 packed into the building."[3] When D. L. Moody died in 1899, Torrey took his place as the national evangelist of the day.

The young boy who had almost ended it all in 1869 was now training hundreds and preaching to thousands. Ed Reece in his

Dr. Torrey preaching in Melbourne, Australia

book of biographies catalogues the ministry of Torrey after Chicago.[4]

"One night Torrey had a strange burden to pray that God would send him around the world with the Gospel. Within a week two strangers from the United Churches of Melbourne, Australia, approached him following a Sunday Service. They told him that they felt he was the man whom God wanted to come to their country for evangelistic services. He accepted."

The meetings in Melbourne propelled Torrey into a worldwide ministry. A former student, Charles M. Alexander, joined him directing his music. Alexander had come from a godly and devout family. He wrote: "My father was an elder in the Presbyterian church. My mother was a consecrated woman, full of deep piety, with a practical strain. At night we would all gather round the fireside, and mother would read Moody's sermons. I remember how we would all break down and cry together over some of his stories."[5]

During this time Alexander won a young man to Christ by the name of Robert Harkness. Harkness was an accomplished musician and was invited to join the team as pianist. Alexander thrilled the great crowds packing the meetings, leading them in *"O That Will Be Glory."*

The Exhibition Building seating 8,000 was filled to capacity each night with 15,000 attempting entry. Ed Reece summarizes the ministry that followed.[6]

Over 20,000 people were converted in Australia and New Zealand. Hundreds came to Christ in meetings in India.

1903 – At Liverpool, England, there were 5000 converts.
1904 – At Dublin, Ireland, 3000 accepted Christ in meetings held at the Metropolitan Hall.
1904 – 30,000 people around the world had committed themselves to pray for the team and worldwide revival.
1904 – (January) Brimingham, England, Campaign held in Bingley Hall saw 7000 professions of faith.
1904 – Cardiff Wales–3,750 saved. (This was the year before Evan Roberts led the Welsh Revival.) Torrey set the stage for that revival.
1904 – (Repeat Campaign) Liverpool, England. A nine-week campaign held in the

Mr. Charles M. Alexander

Tournament Hall seating 12,500–7,000 saved. There were 35,000 turned away on the last day of the meeting for lack of space.
1905 – (February) London, England, Crusade–17,000 professed conversions in meetings held at Royal Albert Hall and other locations. Reece states in his work:[7] "It seemed as though all of London was singing revival hymns. The "Glory Song" (Oh That will be Glory for Me) captured the city led by Alexander and the great choirs."
1905 – Belfast, Northern Ireland – 4000 saved.
1906 – Manchester, England – 4000 saved.
1907 – 1911 – American Crusades in Toronto, Ontario, Atlanta, Ottawa, Ontario, San Francisco, Omaha, Cleveland, Nashville, Buffalo, Montreal, Quebec, Detroit, Los Angeles and Chicago.
1906 – (Spring) Philadelphia– 7000 professed faith in Christ.
1908 – Torrey helped establish the conference ground at Montrose, Pennsylvania.
1911 – More campaigns in England, Scotland and Ireland.

The theme of Torrey's life seemed to have been "Come to Jesus Christ." Torrey gave a Prescription for Revival:

A Prescription That Will Bring Revival

I can give a prescription that will bring revival –revival to any church, or community, or any city on earth.

First: Let a few Christians get thoroughly right with God. If this is not done, the rest will come to nothing.

Second: Let them bind themselves together to pray for revival until God opens the windows of heaven and comes down.

Third: Let them put themselves at the disposal of God for His use as He sees fit in winning others to Christ. That is all. I have given this prescription around the world…and in no instance has it failed.

It cannot fail.

- R. A. Torrey

Torrey attributed the great success to "the people working on the apostolic pattern and upon the plan of God's Model Revival laid down in Acts 2–everyone filled with the Holy Spirit, and everyone going to work."

He authored at least 40 books. As a young preacher I purchased a great book entitled *How To Bring Men To Christ* by R. A. Torrey. Armed with Torrey's Biblical instructions, I led my first soul to Christ.

I left the grave at Montrose that day with a burning heart. As I walked back down the hill from Torrey's grave, I sensed a hunger to know God and His Holy Spirit and power. Had Reuben Torrey committed suicide that night at Yale, how much the world would have missed and how much I would have missed. How much the thousands of Australia would have missed. How much those in England, Scotland, Wales, and other places would have missed.

How much Oswell J. Smith *(converted in the Toronto Crusade 1906)* would have missed and the multitudes influenced by him for missions. How much the students at *Moody Bible Institute* and those influenced by them would have missed. How much *Charles Fuller* (a student of Torrey) would have missed and the millions moved by his *"Old Fashioned Revival Hour Broadcast"* would have missed.

Torrey preached in every major country on earth, touching hundreds of thousands of lives in the process. His name swept London, England, Melbourne, Australia, and the great cities of the world. Modern-day citizens of the small town of Montrose today have no idea of the greatness of the man buried up on the hill. They move about the town to the hardware stores, the businesses, and their homes totally oblivious to one of the greatest lives ever lived…lived in their own little town. Their most celebrated citizen, R. A. Torrey, was the most *famous preacher on earth* less than 100 years ago.

The grave at Montrose lies silent on its windswept hill but multitudes of men, women and children in Heaven rejoice. The grave at Montrose lies silent but the message of Montrose remains the same to all who stop to wonder.

"And ***the world passeth away,*** and the lust thereof: but he that doeth the will of God abideth **Forever!!**" *(1 John 2:17, KJV)*

1 *Torrey and Alexander,* page 22, J. Kennedy MaClean, S. W. Partridge & Company.
2 Ibid.
3 *R. A. Torrey,* page 110, Sword of the Lord Publishers, Murfreesboro, Tennessee.
4 *A Great Cloud of Witnesses,* Ed Reece, Faith Baptist Church Publications, 1996.
5 *Torrey and Alexander,* copyright, 1905 by Fleming H. Revell, Company, New York.

Leicester - City of
F.B.Meyer

I lived in his city. I walked in his steps. I preached in his church. I would love to have known him.

It has been this author's privilege on a number of occasions to speak at Melbourne Hall in Leicester, England. This great church was once pastored by Dr. F. B. Meyer. I will never forget the awesome feeling of standing behind the same pulpit and on the very spot where Meyer stood and preached for so many years of his life. I wish that I could have known him but Leicester made him more real to me than ever before. At Leicester, I preached in his church, saw the cornerstone that he laid and walked the streets that he walked. I identified with Meyer in Leicester. I had moved to Leicester to assist in the planting of a new church and to reach the people for Christ.

One hundred years before, Meyer lived in the city for the same purpose. In Leicester, he poured out his soul to those in darkness. Meyer, writing about his ministry in Leicester, said, *"One of the most popular legends of Brittany is that relating to an imaginary town called 'Is' (pronounced Iss), which is supposed to have been swallowed up by the sea at some unknown time. There are several places along the coast which are pointed out as the site of this city, and the fishermen have many strange tales to tell of it. According to them, the tips of the spires of the churches may be seen in the hollow of the waves when the sea is rough; while during a calm the music of their bells ringing out the hymns rises above the waters.*

Similarly, as it has always seemed to me, amid the submerged masses, deep down at the bottom of the ocean of human life, there are yearnings and desires for a better life, that ring sadly and perpetually. It has been the aim of my life to listen for these, and where I have detected them, to present the only answer—the love of God in Jesus Christ our Lord."[1]

F. B. Meyer had at one time pastored in York. It was there that he met D.L. Moody. Moody and Sankey had arrived from America to discover that the two men who had invited them to England were both dead. A local pastor Fredrick Meyer met Moody and invited him to preach. He then introduced Moody to other pastors. Soon the powerful preaching of D. L. Moody swept through the whole country with thousands of conversions. D. L. Moody imparted to F. B. Meyer a love for souls and evangelism.

Meyer wrote: *"From the beginning of my ministry I had desired to reach the large masses of the people that are outside our churches. This desire was deepened during my pastorate at York, when Moody and Sankey, not then so famous, spent about three weeks with me, preaching those sermons and singing those hymns."*

When Meyer assumed the pastorate at Victoria Road Baptist Church, a large

Through his years in Leicester, F. B. Meyer poured his heart into the city. He was a practical and "people" person.

church in Leicester, he met stiff resistance to his ministry of evangelism. Victoria Road was a society church with paid pews. Those with wealth were assigned special pews. The working class disliked the pew-system, with its class and money distinctions. The affluent members of Victoria Road had little interest and some disdain for common people without class.

Meyer wrote: *"I noticed what large crowds gather in public halls and theaters to hear the simple preaching of God's Word: and I often wished that the time might come when I could preach regularly in a building where all the seats were perfectly open and free to all comers, early attendance alone giving a claim to the same position."* [2]

Meyer's efforts to lead the church into evangelism antagonized the class-conscious members and were blocked by the same. In May of 1878, Meyer resigned as pastor of Victoria Road Baptist Church. However, there were a number of members who had been touched by Meyer's effort to reach others. Relating to this Meyer wrote: *"A number of friends gathered round me and proposed that I should begin preaching to the people in a public hall, the Museum Buildings. Very shortly the place became crowded on Sunday evenings, even to the adjacent room, where people would sit to hear, though they could not see the speaker. Large numbers also professed conversion, and joined the little church."* [3]

On a cold evening in March 1880, about 300 persons gathered to dedicate a piece of ground to God on which a new church building would be erected. In July the memorial stones were laid and on July 2, 1881, the new church, Melbourne Hall, opened its doors for the first service. The building would seat 1300. When the pews were filled, chairs were placed in the aisle bringing the capacity to 2000. The church had 80 workers and sometimes ministered to 2500 in Sunday School. *I lived in his city. I walked in his steps. I preached in his church. I would love to have known him.*

During the same years the old church, Victoria Road, which had rejected Meyer's evangelistic leadership, grew weaker and weaker. Finally to survive, the church merged with another Baptist church in the city, leaving their large and glorious building. Today a cult group uses the building, while Melbourne Hall continues to flourish.

Through his years in Leicester, F. B. Meyer poured his heart into the city.

Dr. Meyer in front of Melbourne Hall Church

He was a practical and "people" person. He developed a prison ministry that changed many lives. He had noticed that when men were discharged at the prison gate on Monday morning, many of them whose families did not meet them returned to the beer house across the street from the prison. There they would begin again the cycle that had led them to prison in the first place.

Meyer made it his business to wait at the prison gate for these men. He offered to take them to the coffee house instead of the beer house. There he would feed them and witness to them of Christ. Hundreds were converted in this way. He would encourage them to sign a pledge not to drink again. The great problem that these former prisoners faced was that of employment. No one wanted to hire an ex-con. Eventually, Meyer organized business enterprises to give these men work. First, there was the *F. B. Meyer Firewood Merchant*. With Meyer's name attached, people bought the wood readily. This was followed by the Window-Cleaning Brigade. Commenting on this enterprise, Meyer wrote: *"It was said, a little unfairly, that a man must get into prison before I would do anything to help him. After considerable cogitation, I bought a ladder or two, some buckets, and started one or two men on the job of window-cleaning. Cards, on which my name was printed, which guaranteed their respectability, were left from door to door, to be followed up a day or two after. On the same line, and to give employment to the same class, I started the Messenger Brigade. This was intended more especially to help old men who were no longer fit for*

Victoria Road Baptist Church in Leicester, England

laborious work. We began with four, in different parts of the town. They stood at certain spots, waiting to be sent on errands, to be called in to polish boots, or do any odd jobs about the house. They wore a specially-made hat with my name in the front, and were paid so much per quarter of an hour, or per quarter of a mile, keeping all they earned" [4]

On Saturday evening he and fellow Christians would go through the streets of Leicester looking for people to help. Many overcome by drink would be helped home and given a Gospel witness. On one occasion when Dr. Meyer preached at a small chapel, a man approached him. The man shook and kissed Dr. Meyer's hand. F. B. Meyer commenting on this wrote: "I confess that it made a choking sensation come to my throat." The man was one whom Meyer had "met at the gate" of the prison. He was now redeemed and was an active Christian. Dr. Meyer had not only saved his soul but had also saved his life.

F. B. Meyer was foremost a preacher but he was also a public campaigner against sin. He sat on the city council and was partly responsible for closing 400 immoral places.

Meyer's advice to young ministers was: *"Mix freely with the people; visit systematically and widely; study men as well as books; converse with all classes and conditions of men: always on the alert to learn from some fresh pages of the heart."* [5]

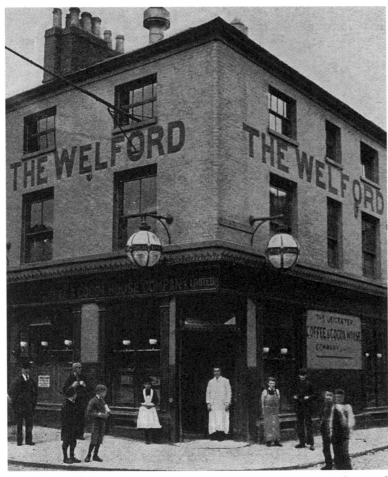

The Welford Coffee House, Leicester. F.B. Meyer would meet prisoners at the gate of Leicester prison upon their release and bring them to this location. Here he would feed them and win them to Christ.

Edna Knight

I lived in his city. I walked in his steps. I preached in his church. I would love to have known him. God moved me a step closer to that dream by sending Mrs. Edna Knight to our church. Mrs. Knight had at one time been a member of a church pastored by F. B. Meyer. Edna was nearly 90 years old when she discovered our church. She had been attending another church in the city. One morning on her way to church, she walked by our church, heard the singing and ventured in. Lifegate Baptist Church was what she had been searching for. Later she told me that she had known Dr. Meyer and had taught a Sunday School class at his church. In a recorded interview that this author had with Edna Knight some years ago, she related the following: *"During the First World War when I was about 16 years old, I attended F. B. Meyer's church. That was when he pastured at Westminster Bridge Road. During that time I taught a Sunday School class at the church. When the war ended, Dr. Meyer held a special service to honor those who had fought for our freedom. The British and American flags were displayed in the church that day. There was a special place where the American soldiers were assigned for seating. All the soldiers marched in taking their place. It was a touching service. I expressed a desire to become a member of Dr. Meyer's church. Although I had been converted some years earlier, Dr. Meyer took nothing for granted. He took me by the hand, looked into my eyes and asked, 'Are you sure? Are you really sure that you have received Jesus Christ into your life?' Of course I was, but I always remembered those words spoken to me by F. B. Meyer. To him following Jesus Christ was far more than simply becoming a member of the church. Dr. Meyer was very much a gentleman in the pulpit and out. He was always so earnest, very sincere and genuine."*

Edna Knight

Amazingly, Edna Knight had been a member of both F. B. Meyer's church and also G. Campbell Morgan's church at different times. I asked Edna: *"Mrs. Knight, when you sat under the ministry of these two great preachers, Dr. F. B. Meyer and Dr. Campbell Morgan, what did you feel?"* She replied, *"I felt the Spirit of God. They made me glad that I had come. It has been long ago but I can still remember the spirit of those meetings. I'll tell you how long it has been. I was on my way to Dr. Meyer's services one Sunday and saw on the placard at the newsstand these headlines, 'THE TITANIC HAS SUNK!' I can still see that headline. Everyone in London was in shock over this."*

Continuing the conversation, I asked, "Mrs. Knight, you are 90 years old. Just for the record, let me ask how active you are able to be in the ministry of your church?" "I attend Sunday morning,

Sunday evening, Wednesday evening and go out witnessing on visitation each Wednesday morning," was the reply.

At 90 years, Edna Knight continued to live the life for Christ instilled in her as a child by Dr. F. B. Meyer. F. B. Meyer died in 1929. As his body was carried out of the church, the congregation sang the *Hallelujah Chorus* and F. B. Meyer moved out of his church… for the last time.

*I lived in his city. I walked in his steps. I preached in his church. I would love to have known him…**and now…I think I do.***

1 *The Bells of Is.* By F. B. Meyer, (London: Morgan and Scott).
2 *The Bells of Is.* By F. B. Meyer, (London: Morgan and Scott).
3 Ibid.
4 Ibid. Meyer, 98.
5 Ibid.

In Search of...
John Knox

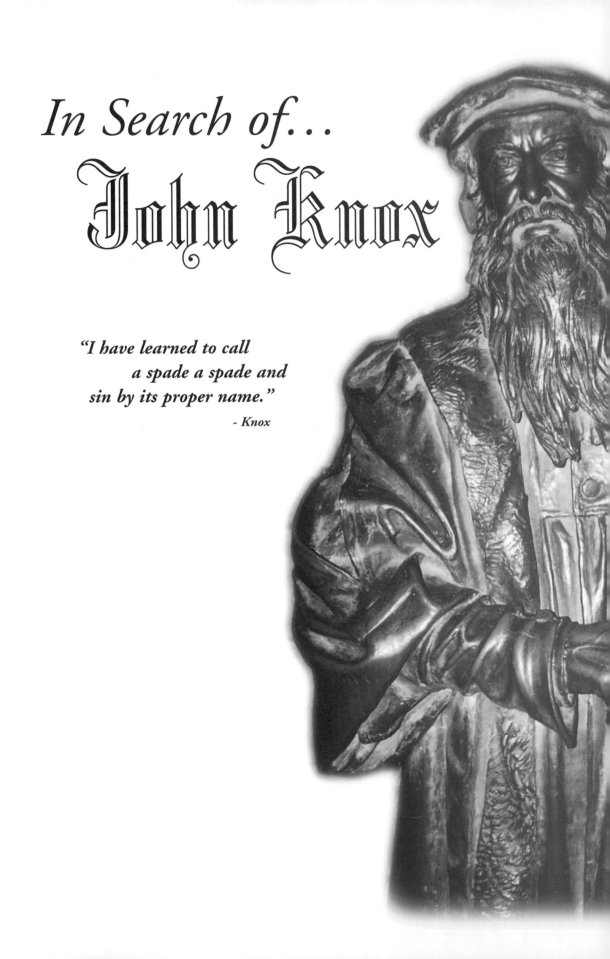

*"I have learned to call
a spade a spade and
sin by its proper name."*

- Knox

"GIVE ME SCOTLAND OR I DIE."

These famous words were the heart cry of John Knox, the Prophet of Edinburgh. That cry was very suitable in the days of Knox, for Scotland with its Catholic Queen stood in grave danger. Mary Queen of Scots was a Catholic but her nation was Protestant. It would only be a matter of time, a few thousand martyrs, a measure of conspiracy, and the doctrine of popery would be well entrenched.

I felt sadness as I walked over the parking lot adjoining the church where Knox preached and ministered. He lies buried in that parking lot with only a small square marking his final resting place. It was unimaginable to think that the man who saved Scotland is no more honored than to have muddy automobile tires rolling over his grave daily.

There was a time when the name John Knox was synonymous with Edinburgh. Knox, the most outspoken preacher of his day, ministered in the most important city of the country. Today Scotland does not glory in John Knox.

The mainstream religious elements in the country are ecumenical, with some exceptions. Modern church fathers have little interest in a past radical who coined the phrase *"I have learned to call a spade a spade and sin by its proper name."* Indeed the Scots, as a whole, would rather forget John Knox–especially that for which he stood.

After all, Edinburgh can boast of many sons. A few blocks away from Princess

John Knox,

from begining to end,

was a preacher and

so it was he died.

Street still stands a house once inhabited by the Bells. A plaque on it reads "ALEXANDER GRAHAM BELL–Inventor of the Telephone."

Just three years after the birth of Bell, another birth was recorded in the city–Robert Louis Stevenson, destined to become a famous essayist, novelist, and poet. The childhood home of Stevenson can still be seen at 17 Reriot Row. Growing up in Edinburgh, Stevenson absorbed the city. He had a great interest in the Covenanters who went to their noble deaths in the Grassmarket. Their courage intrigued him all of his life. He was born here March 3, 1847.

One would have thought that of all heroes of Edinburgh's past, John Knox would have been the most revered. There were the old homeplaces of Bell, Stevenson, Sir Walter Scott, and others; but Knox–where were his memorials?

In time I did discover memorials to Knox. His house still stands and is gratefully a fitting memorial open to the public. St. Giles Church still stands where Knox faithfully preached the Gospel of Christ.

Edinburgh and Scotland possibly owe more to Knox than any other single past leader, yet today he is the least honored. Recently his statue was brought inside St. Giles Church and placed in an obscure corner.

I will never forget the day I first saw the grave of John Knox. The man who saved Scotland is not so honored as poet Sir Walter Scott. Scott's enormous memorial on Princess Street, larger than some churches, contains his larger than life statue seated as if on a throne.

My emotions turned to anger and then sadness as I viewed the only marker commemorating the final resting-place of Knox–a small gold colored square of concrete in the car park near St. Giles Church. With each passing day people unknowingly trample under foot the grave of the "Man who Saved Scotland" from a Catholic bloodbath.

If John Knox were famous for his boldness, he was renowned for his preaching. While some men of the reformation were great teachers and writers, Knox was a preacher. It was said that "Others snipped at the branches but this man strikes at the root."

The Reformer was born in the year *1505* in Haddington, East Lothian. His father was a farmer. Most of what is known about him dates from the year 1546. These were momentous days for Scotland. The country held an alliance with France, having developed close communication with the Continent. The Bible had been translated into the common tongue. Patrick Hamilton, a great light from God, was martyred. The death of Hamilton along with other martyrs made a deep impression on the young Knox.

George Wishart, later martyred, preached throughout Scotland with his last message preached at Haddington. A companion stood next to him with a two-handed sword to protect him. The companion was the priest turned reformer John Knox.

If John Knox were famous for his boldness, he was renowned for his preaching. It was said that "Others snipped at the branches but this man strikes at the root."

Mary Queen of Scots

Knox, a confirmed

Protestant, was involved

in a long series of

confrontations with

Mary Queen of Scots,

a devout Roman Catholic

and the ruler of Scotland.

The burning of George Wishart left a fire burning in the heart of Knox.

It was the preaching of Knox that frightened Queen Mary most. Sometimes those sermons caused riots. Always, they motivated the hearers to stand against popery.

Two outstanding events characterized the year *1561*. Mary Queen of Scots landed to assume the throne of Scotland and John Knox was made Minister in Edinburgh. Queen Mary was a Roman Catholic. Knox was a confirmed Protestant. The first Sunday after Mary's arrival she held mass in the palace, while up the street a few blocks away Knox thundered against the idolatry of the mass.

A long series of confrontations followed. On several occasions Knox was called before the Queen to answer for his sermons and actions. His piercing answers often left her enraged and sobbing. Mary had Knox arrested and tried for treason but he was acquitted. It was the ministry of this Prophet of Edinburgh that unveiled the duplicitious plots of Queen Mary and her Catholic agents. Later she fled to England where Queen Elizabeth I eventually ordered her execution.

John Knox, from beginning to end, was a preacher and so it was he died. The most memorable picture of him depicts him leaning over the pulpit preaching. I have wondered many times what reaction he would have to the present day ecumenical circles. If John Knox lived in Edinburgh today, this city would know it. The ecumenical crowd would not have a Sunday's peace while Knox was in town.

Scotland today needs men of the stature of John Knox to boldly proclaim the Word of God. Only a holy boldness of a John Knox can make a dent in the darkness of this hour.

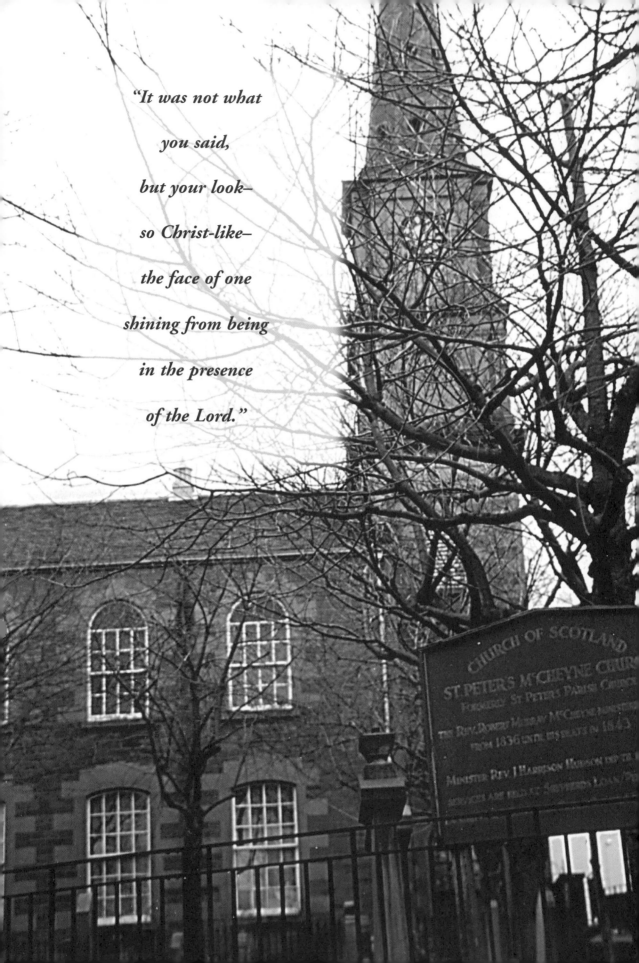

"It was not what

you said,

but your look—

so Christ-like—

the face of one

shining from being

in the presence

of the Lord."

The Weeping Prophet of Scotland

Robert Murray M'Cheyne

AFTER THE DEATH of Robert Murray M'Cheyne, a visiting American minister asked the caretaker of St. Peter's Church if he might see M'Cheyne's pulpit. After walking through the beautiful sanctuary, he then asked if he might walk up into the pulpit. The caretaker gave permission.

He stood at the spot and meditated on the great preacher of days past. Then the caretaker, who had actually known M'Cheyne, shouted, *"Now sir... WEEP...WEEP for SOULS...WEEP like M'Cheyne wept."*

ROBERT MURRAY M'Cheyne was born in Edinburgh May 21, 1813. It was there that he was educated at the high school and university and gained distinction in his classes. Professor Wilson North awarded him the poetry prize. The Presbytery of Annan licensed him in 1835. His first sermon was preached in Ruthwell Church. It was November 24, 1836, that he was ordained to St. Peter's Church at Dundee, Scotland.

In 1839, M'Cheyne visited Palestine for the purpose of promoting a mission to the Jews. On his return to Dundee, he threw himself heart and soul into revival work in that city. Twice he visited the north of Ireland and often preached evangelistic meetings in other areas of Scotland.

M'Cheyne's ministry in Dundee was remarkable. Some Sundays he conducted extra services to accommodate the crowds who came to hear him. M'Cheyne had the ability to lead men. His personal magnetism enabled him to lead others to work with him in many endeavors. He surrounded himself with office-bearers that shared responsibility.

A large staff of tract distributors was organized. There were large Sabbath Schools and also something like we would now call a children's church.

Church in Dundee where M'Cheyne poured out his life for souls

"The service did not take place in the church but in the Newton graveyard, some distance from the building. It was a remarkable open-air service. M'Cheyne's subject was the Great White Throne. He continued preaching till the sun set behind the mountain tops of Arran, across the sea."

The account described in detail the impact of that hour. As the darkness fell, M'Cheyne compared the shadows with the setting of time and the ending of life. Soon the speaker could not be seen for the darkness but the power of God was present as the preaching continued.

The voice of M'Cheyne penetrated the blackness with a burning earnestness that stirred the congregation. Through the darkness came the pleading voice of the preacher as if it were the voice of God Himself.

The witness continued, *"His lips were touched with the live coal from the altar... HE BELIEVED WHAT HE SPOKE; and everything to him was as nothing—but loss —that he might win souls to Christ."*

M'Cheyne was not an orator like Chalmers or Guthrie. He preached with remarkable simplicity—straight to the mind and straight to the heart.

After his death there was found in his desk a letter sent to him by a stranger who had attended a service of his church. The writer described his impression, stating that **it was not so much what he said in his sermon**

St. Peters was known for a variety of Christian enterprises and the number of its workers. In a day when Jews were despised throughout many countries, M'Cheyne poured out his heart for their souls. Foreign missions were a large part of his pulpit emphasis.

Few preachers living today have matched M'Cheyne's love for the Word of God. In his mere 30 years of life he read the Bible through some 100 times. This habit with the Word had a profound effect upon his ministry and life.

From the pulpit he proclaimed a message of revival. *"Let preachers preach up the standards of the church and let dead preaching come to an end. Reformation in the lives of ministers, preaching more by their holy and consistent lives than their sermons."*

On one occasion he preached in Ayrshire. This service was never forgotten by those in attendance. Years afterward one who was present that day related his experience.

as much as the **LOOK ON THE PREACHER'S FACE.** The visitor wrote: *"It was not what you said, but your look– so Christ-like–the face of one shining from being in the presence of the Lord."* M'Cheyne LIVED the Christian life. He shone not only in the pulpit but also in everyday life.

Professor Stalker of Aberdeen recounted this event. "In Alexandria, Egypt, a lady happened to be staying at one of the hotels there. Something had irritated her, and she launched forth against professing Christians as just a lot of hypocrites. She would not believe any of them. They would cheat whenever and wherever they could. 'Well,' said one who was patiently listening to the tirade, 'did you never in all your life meet one Christian, ONE FOLLOWER of the Lord in whom you had confidence?'

There was a pause. Then the lady, in a soft tone said, 'Yes, I saw one–a minister in this hotel, a tall, lean fellow from Scotland. He was a man of God. I watched him, and felt that he was a genuine Christian. His very look made me feel good.' That minister was **Robert M'Cheyne.**" His holy, consistent life was telling a story in that hotel among people he had never seen before and whom likely he would never see again.

Dr. Baxter said of M'Cheyne: *"He was one of the most complete ministers I ever met. He was a great peacemaker, an excellent visitor, a complete Christian. He visited the dying on Saturday so that his heart might be touched by what he saw, so that on Sunday, when he preached, he would preach with tenderness."*

McCheyne went on an evangelistic tour of the northeast of Scotland after which he returned much fatigued. A few days later he was seized with fever and died March 25, 1843. The emblem which he used on his printed material and had painted on his watch had been the setting sun. When the sun set in Dundee, Scotland, that day in March of 1843, it had carried with it the greatest preacher that Dundee had ever had. His tomb stands just feet away from the pulpit separated only by the church walls.

Andrew Bonar said, *"There is still a peculiar fragrance in the air at Robert M'Cheyne's tomb."*

For years now the church has remained empty. The Free Church of Scotland purchased the building and again services will be held there. Dundee, with all of its church steeples, is in need of ANOTHER WEEPING PROPHET. The voice of M'Cheyne has long been silent. In addition to existing Gospel witness, there is a need of more evangelism in the city today.

Robert Murrey M'Cheyne, even by the inscription on his tomb, cast his shadow over modern-day Christians who have lost their way in a maze of selfishness.

"HE CEASED NOT day or night to labor and watch for souls; and was honored by His Lord to draw many wanderers out of darkness into the path of life."

> *Through the darkness came the pleading voice of the preacher as if it were the voice of God Himself.*

A Pilgrim
In Search of a City!

The story of Pilgrim's Progress is the story of John Bunyan. The main character in the story is he, himself, a pilgrim in search of heaven, leaving the city of destruction.

"**A**s I walked through the wilderness of this world, I lighted on a certain place where was a den, and I laid me down in that place to sleep. And as I slept, I dreamed a dream." These statements begin the allegory and dream of three hundred years ago. Other than the Bible, *Pilgrim's Progress* has been classified as the world's greatest story. The dreams of John Bunyan have blessed the world for 300 years.

I was 17 years old when I first heard of *Pilgrim's Progress*. The teacher of literature at Fort Valley High, sensing that I had some religious interest, suggested that I should read it and report on it. Those students that valued life did not cross Mrs. Thelma Wilson. If she suggested a book to you, you dared not procrastinate. She ran her classroom like a U.S. Army boot camp and the day of accountability would come.

Mrs. Wilson introduced me not only to one of the greatest books ever written but also to the author John Bunyan. Little did I know back then in 1957 that I would one day walk in the very tracks of the great man in far away England.

John Bunyan was born near Elstow Village, a few miles from Bedford, England, in 1628. The old parish church that he attended as a child still stands in the village. The graves of Bunyan's parents are found among the tombs in the cemetery surrounding the church. When John was a young man, he volunteered to ring the church bells that announced the services. The bell tower, a separate structure, still stands today a few feet away from the church. John pulled on the ropes, tugging the bells from one side to the other. Looking up at the huge iron bells, he envisioned one of them falling on him and killing him. Also John was a reckless and wild young man. He admitted having few equals of his age for cursing, swearing, lying and blaspheming the holy name of God. Fearing God's judgment from a falling church bell, he gave up bell ringing.

John Bunyan was 16 years old when his mother died. This great sorrow was compounded a month later when his sister, whom he loved, also died and was carried out to the grave. After serving in the army, Bunyan returned to Elstow in 1647. Soon afterward he married a girl named Mary, whose surname history has not

Elstow Village, near Bedford, England, childhood home of John Bunyan

recorded. Mary was from a Godly family and exerted a good influence on John. The couple loved each other dearly. God was at work in John Bunyan's life.

The Reverend John Gifford was a newly appointed pastor of an independent congregation which met at St. John's Church. Under his ministry in 1653, John Bunyan was converted and brought to a personal faith in Jesus Christ. Gifford spent many hours with Bunyan teaching him the Bible. The old manse in which Gifford lived next to St. John's church still exists today. Later in Bunyan's famous story he tells of a man called "Evangelist" who pointed Pilgrim on his way. Without doubt it was his mentor Gifford who inspired the character of "Evangelist."

Two tragedies came into his life at this time. The first was the birth of his little daughter Mary born blind. The second tragedy was the death of his young wife. Life now became a very serious matter to him. God must have His way at last.

Eventually, Bunyan married a beautiful lady known as Elizabeth. By the time of this marriage he had become a devout Christian and by 1657 was preaching. His ministry in the Bedford and surrounding villages was attracting wide attention. Great crowds came to hear him preach. Many open air meetings were held in the Bedford square with hundreds attending. The attendance at his Baptist church in Bedford now numbered up to 1000 people. In that day the entire population of the city numbered only 2000 people. The once vile and wretched Bunyan, now as a preacher of the Gospel, commanded the attention of half the population of Bedford.

There was no small stir when Bunyan, now well known and respected by half the population, was arrested for illegal preaching. King Charles II had landed in England in May of 1660 to reclaim the throne. To unify the country religiously, a law had been passed known as the law of uniformity. The idea was to unify all religious activity thus unifying the country. Non-conformist preaching would be illegal. F. T. Wells in his work on Bunyan describes the events that led to the preacher's arrest: *"Bunyan carried on with his evangelism in spite of grave dangers and, on the twelfth of November 1660, went to the tiny hamlet of lower Samsell near Harlington to hold a service. As soon as he arrived he knew that something was wrong for the assembled congregation was fearful and apprehensive. The farmer, in whose house the service was to be held, took John aside and told him of the warrant already made out for his arrest, urging him to fly while there was still time. John would hear nothing of this, fearing it would be a sorry example to any convert should he run away at the first sign of danger."* [1]

The service began but was soon interrupted by the magistrate who arrested Bunyan for illegal preaching. Being led away, he begged the people not to be discouraged.

When John was brought to trial, the judge hearing the case realized that no serious crime had been committed. However, a law had been broken. Preaching outside the Church of England was now illegal. He offered Bunyan his freedom if he would promise to refrain from any further "illegal" preaching. Bunyan replied to the judge, "If I am released from jail today, I will be preaching again tomorrow."

That statement made when he was 32 years old cost John Bunyan 12 years of his life. Although the prison terms were in increments, the years rolled into 12. For 12 years he lingered in a stinking, vile and crowded jail in Bedford, England. For the sake of the Gospel, he gave up 12 years of life with his wife and children. For 12 years he languished in a vile place. For 12 years he was growing old in prison while his children grew up. For 12 years he suffered isolation in darkness and confinement away from the blooming flowers and sunshine. He watched 12 summers, 12 autumns, 12 winters and 12 springtimes slip past. For 12 years his wife, Elizabeth, cooked his meals and sent them by Mary, his blind daughter. For 12 years the little blind girl made her way through the streets of the city to the prison with his food.

Bunyan was alone, depressed and persecuted. It was during this confinement in Bedford Jail that John Bunyan discovered a *secret power* that saw him through. Picking up his pen, he wrote the world's most famous story, of a man, a pilgrim living in a city of destruction, seeking God.

What most people do not know is that *Pilgrim's Progress* is Bunyan's own testimony of his search for God and his persecution as a preacher. The places in the story are literal places around Bedford. The *slough of despond* was an actual swamp near the city. The people in the story were people he actually knew. In *Pilgrim's Progress*, Mr. Hategood was (in real life) the judge who refused to release him and who showed no mercy at his trial.

The story of *Pilgrim's Progress* is the story of John Bunyan. The main character in the story is he, himself, a pilgrim in search of heaven, leaving the city of destruction. In the story, Pilgrim on his way to the Celestial City wanders on to the grounds of Doubting Castle, owned by a Giant called Despair. He is captured and thrown into the Dungeon of Giant Despair. Giant Despair showed Pilgrim the bones of other pilgrims whom he, Giant Despair, had slain. For many days Pilgrim languished in the dungeon of Giant Despair in Doubting Castle. Then one day it dawned upon him that he had a key in his bosom that would open every door in the castle. The key was the promises of God.

In Bunyan's real world Giant Despair was his jailkeeper. *Doubting Castle* was none

Grave of John Bunyan – BunHill Fields, London, Englnd

other than *Bedford Jail*. There in that dreadful place, John Bunyan laid hold of the promises of God. The promises of God lifted his spirit and gave him hope to go on and on.

After 12 years Bunyan was released, but he remained under constant threat from the authorities for the remainder of his life. In all of his troubles he never flinched. The religious establishment in league with legal authorities had locked the Baptist preacher up to silence him. However, *Pilgrim's Progress*, written in Bedford Prison, has preached the gospel that Bunyan preached around the world for 300 years. *Pilgrim's Progress* has been translated into more than 166 languages. These are more languages than are represented in the British Museum.

John Bunyan is buried at BunHill Fields Cemetery off City Road in London. BunHill Fields is the author's favorite cemetery. Walking through that cemetery, I have seen the graves of the separatists including Susanna Wesley, Isaac Watts, John Gill and yes…**John Bunyan**.

John Bunyan lived 10 years beyond his release from Bedford Jail. In spite of the fact that his writings had made him famous, the authorities were still observing him. He had traveled to London for a preaching engagement. While in the city he caught pneumonia and died. There in London a suffering, persecuted servant of God who had traveled through a vale of darkness had at last reached the land of light. The pilgrim had at last crossed over the river and entered the Celestial City which he had so long envisioned.

London was not the end of John Bunyan's story, for multitudes have read it and gained hope in darkness. Untold numbers of Christians through the ages have gathered strength from its pages to go on in spite of persecution and affliction. To believers today, the writings of John Bunyan, written over 300 years ago, hold out to us that same secret power…and when DESPAIR comes upon us like a GIANT, we too can lay hold of *the promises of God!*

It was during this confinement in Bedford Jail that John Bunyan discovered a secret power that saw him through. Picking up his pen, he wrote the world's most famous story, of a man, a pilgrim living in a city of destruction, seeking God.

---

1 *Story of John Bunyan Museum*, F. T. Wells, Viking Lithoprint, Bedford, England.

"The world marches

forth on the feet of

little children."
- Robert Raikes

Encounter with...

Robert Raikes

y wife and I held on to our seats as the executive of the Coco-Cola Company sped his car around London giving us a quick tour. Peter drove his car through the busy streets with ease and confidence. This was his domain. He fit well into the London scene with his pin-stripped shirt, posh London accent and knowledge of the area. Pointing out the Parliament, Westminster Abbey and the Tower Bridge, Peter then turned a corner and sped along the banks of the Thames. "That was Robert Raikes, the founder of the Sunday School," he said as we zoomed past a stature.

That was my first encounter with Robert Raikes…but not my last. I would not rest until I knew more of a man who made a difference in the lives of MILLIONS! Following the path of Raikes led me back into the 18th century and into a world unknown to the millions in England today. C.B. Eavey in his work on Christian education described the condition of the times: *The physical, intellectual, and moral conditions of the masses in Raikes' day were deplorable. People lived in dwellings rudely put together. Often geese, chickens, and pigs occupied the same premises. The people wore coarse clothing, existed on a very poor diet, and slept on straw. In industrial cities like Gloucester conditions were especially bad. There was no system of public education. Few common people had the privilege of attending even an elementary school. It was not easy to find a poor man who could read. Ignorance and vice, dissipation and ungodliness prevailed, especially among the lower classes. The ruling class attempted to control vice and crime by means of drastic laws and severe penalties. As a result, prisons were filled with people*

of all types, from confirmed criminals to respectable persons who were imprisoned because they could not pay their debts." [1]

During those years the children of England were little more than "white slaves." They worked long, weary hours in the mills and factories which were little more than sweatshops. Their day began before daylight and ended after dark. In 1847 Parliament passed a child labor law that stated that

> ## *"The physical, intellectual, and moral conditions of the masses in Raikes' day were deplorable."*

"CHILDREN COULD WORK NO MORE THAN TEN HOURS PER DAY." Twelve hours had been the norm.

The Industrial Revolution was in the process of dismantling the village crafts in favor of the smoky, dingy but mass-producing factories. Thousands were leaving the villages and flooding into the cities. Very often there was no place for the immigrants from the countryside in the churches of the industrialized towns. [2] Sunday was the only day of release for the horde of children. Let loose on that day from their toil, they roamed the streets playing, cursing and fighting. These children were abandoned by parents and society at large to engage in whatever vices they could find.

On to this page of history there stepped Robert Raikes to make a difference in the lives of these abandoned people. Raikes had a noble heritage. Both of his grandfathers, Richard Drew and Timothy Raikes, were ministers. Robert's father, Robert Sr., was a newspaper publisher and he used that position to campaign against the wretched conditions of the poor.

Robert (II) enrolled at the cathedral school when he was fourteen and from his father learned the business of publishing. He was thirty-one when he married Anne Trigge from the nearby village of Newnham. Robert and Anne had ten children with eight surviving to adulthood.

After the death of his father, Robert became editor of the family newspaper, the *Gloucester Journal.* James Reed describes a man with a vision to make a difference.

"From the beginning of his editorship, Raikes used his newspaper as a means for helping those he found naked, starving, and rotting in jails. He begged for them, he followed them when they were deported, and he sought to impress upon the minds of his readers concern for unfortunate people. He championed the poor, who were unable to afford the rising cost of wheat and became involved in teaching them to read and write."[3]

The children of Gloucester now caught the eye of Robert Raikes. He saw them on Sundays running wild in the streets of moral filth. He knew it would do little good to try to persuade the parents to control their children. Indeed the parents had never known anything

Raikes wanted to build something into the children they could not get in their homes— character! The first Sunday School would be not only a Sunday School... but a school.

different themselves. Raikes knew to make a difference he would have to start with the children themselves.

English law made it illegal for persons outside the Church of England to have schools. In 1779 Parliament passed the *Enabling Act,* which legalized other schools. Acting immediately, Raikes started his first Sunday School in 1780. The location was the kitchen of a Mrs. Meredith who lived in Sooty Alley (so named because many of the chimney sweeps lived there). Robert Raikes intended to teach these children to read and write and to use the Bible as a textbook.

Raikes wanted to build something into the children they could not get in their homes— character! The first Sunday School would be not only a Sunday School...but a school. This presented a wonderful opportunity for children from the lowest level of society who knew nothing but poverty and hard work. The school was opened for children from age six to fourteen.

Raikes felt that standards were necessary for good order. Although the children's clothes were ragged, they were required to come with clean hands and face and combed hair. The children were in class on Sunday from ten to twelve in the morning. They went home and returned at one o'clock. After a lesson they were then taken to church. After church they were taught the Bible until five o'clock.

Those who were well behaved were presented with awards such as Bibles, Testaments, books and clothing.

The lesson vocabulary came from the Bible. By lesson thirty-eight the children were pronouncing words such as: "O-be-di-ent," "Co-vet-ous," "trans-gres-sion." The question and answer method was used for teaching.

Question: Did the world make itself?

Answer: No; if that clock had a maker, much more the world had a maker.

Question: How do you prove that there is a God?

Answer: First, by common sense; second, by our conscience; third, by tradition; forth, by the Sabbath, and fifth, by the Scriptures. Raikes once commented, "Conscience proves that there is a God as a constable who serves us with a warrant proves there is a magistrate."

Question: How do you prove the truth of the Gospel or that Jesus Christ was the Son of God?

Answer: By the miracles that He wrought and the prophecies which can be fulfilled.[4]

Robert Raikes was a born leader of men. He organized, deputized and supervised. He hired people to teach and supervised the activity, making sure that all went as planned.

The change in the children and the city was astounding. Five years after Raikes began that first Sunday School, one minister of the times observing the Sunday School remarked: "The children, who from being savage and filthy in their manners and appearance, are now becoming decent, orderly, and attentive to cleanliness."[5]

The farmers, the manufacturers, and the businesses that hired the children were amazed at the improvement. One manufacturer of hemp and flax, who employed a great number of children, compared the change in the children from that of a "tiger to men."

Gloucester, Raikes' own city, was impressed. In 1786, six years after Raikes started the Sunday School, the city leaders passed a unanimous vote of thanks for the accomplishment. In 1792, twelve years after the start not one criminal

The teaching of the Bible lifted the standard of morality out of the gutter in Raikes' day. Transported to early America, it became the foundation of morality and integrity.

defendant appeared before the judge; ten years earlier there would have been anywhere between ten and one hundred cases.[6] Raikes launched a campaign to begin other schools. The movement caught on affecting thousands of lives across the country.

There arose some opposition. In Scotland the Rev. Thomas Burns criticized with "I am afraid that these Sunday Schools will in the end destroy all family religion. These schools are hurtful to public religion."[7]

The *Imperial Magazine* expressed opposition with these words: "Religion will neither fill our bellies nor clothe our bodies, and, as to reading, it only serves to render poor folks proud and idle."[8] Even Raikes own brother, a minister, criticized him for not giving more credit to other workers.

Robert Raikes was undeterred but he felt the criticisms deeply. Writing to Lewelyn in May 1790, he says, *"I did not conceive that I held any degree of esteem among my neighbors, and am, therefore, the more*

Statue of Robert Raikes, founder of the first Sunday School in 1780

astonished of our having heard anything praise-worthy of one that here seems to be walking alone. I can prevail on no one to second me in my little efforts to civilize the long-despised and neglected children of indigence. It seems as if I had discovered a new country, where no other adventurer chooses to follow. It is some reward for the scorn and contempt of my neighbors that I am frequently honored by visits from strangers....[9]

Robert Raikes, however, was not alone. John Wesley and other leaders praised him. In time the Queen herself called for an interview with Raikes and gave him her support. By 1984 there were 2,000 children attending Sunday Schools in Leeds alone with 250,000 in the whole country.[10] A Parliamentary return in 1818 gave a total of 477, 225, more than 4% of the entire population. In 1833 the number had increased to over a million and a half and in 1851 to over two million, being 13% of the population.

In the United States the movement was propelled throughout the whole nation. One leading minister in 1848 declared in a letter to a friend, *"America has practically been saved for Christianity and the religion of the Bible by the Sunday School."*

It is a sad commentary today that the American Government of this day has degenerated to a state where many of those in leadership believe that God, the Bible and the church have no part to play in education. What public schools there were in Raikes' day used the Bible as a textbook. The teaching of the Bible lifted the standard of morality out of the gutter in Raikes' day. Transported to early America, it became the foundation of morality and integrity. Great universities such as Harvard and Cambridge were founded originally on its precepts. Some thirty years after the establishment of Raikes' first Sunday School, Joseph Lancaster visited Raikes. Gregory in his work recounts the scene: *"Raikes took Lancaster, who was an educational reformer himself, to the spot in a back Alley. Turning to Lancaster, Raikes said, 'Pause here.' Then, uncovering his head and closing his eyes, he stood for a moment in silent prayer. Then turning towards his friend, while the tears rolled down his cheeks he said: 'This is the spot on which I stood when I saw the destitution of the children and the desecration of the Sabbath by the inhabitants of the city. As I asked 'Can nothing be done?' a voice answered 'Try.' I did try, and see what God has wrought. I can never pass by the spot where the word, 'try' came so powerfully into my mind without lifting up my hands and heart to Heaven in gratitude to God for having put such a great thought into my heart."* [11]

It was April 5, 1811, when some beautiful little children gathered again around Robert Raikes. He had died suddenly of a heart attack. His daughter described the scene. "Some of the scholars—the girls wearing white bonnets with black strings—waited in the Crypt Alley for the funeral procession, which preceded to the church."

They sang for him one last time. Raikes had planned it this way. He wanted the children whom he had loved in life to surround him in death. Nor had he forgotten the "little rewards." Each child was to receive a shilling and a plum cake.

He was buried in the Church of St. Mary de Crypt. The memorial to Raikes reads:

Sacred to the memory of

ROBERT RAIKES, Esq.,

(late of this city)

Founder of Sunday Schools

Who departed this life

April 5th, 1811, Age 75 years.

"When the ear heard me, then it blessed me; and when the eye saw me, it gave witness to me: because I delivered the poor that cried, and the fatherless, and him that had none to help him. The blessing of him that was ready to perish came upon me, and I caused the widow's heart to sing for joy."

Job. 29: 11-13

The millions who attend Sunday School today across the world know little of Robert Raikes but they have come to know his God. The world still marches forth…on the…"Feet of Little Children!"

---

1 *History of Christian Educations*, C.B. Eavey, p. 223, Moody Press, Chicago 1964.

2 *Glimpses*, Issue 34, Gospel Communications Network.

3 *A History of Christian Education*, p. 256, James E. Reed and Ronnie Prevost, Broadman & Holman Publishers 1993.

4 *Robert Raikes*, by Guy Kendall, Nicholson and Watson Ltd. London 1939.

5 *In a Sermon preached on behalf of the Sunday Schools*, January 3, 1785.

6 *Glimpses*, issue #34, Christian History Institute.

7 *Harris*, p. 199.

8 *Harris Longer Life*, p. 90.

9 *Robert Raikes*, by Guy Kendall, Nicholson & Watson Ltd. London, 1939.

10 *Gentlemen's Magazine*, November 1787.

11 *Gregory*, pp. 144-5.

Aldergate Street

John Wesley

I was amazed that the monument at Altergate was still there. In the heart of the modern paganism of London, it had survived among high-rise buildings and modern construction. John Wesley may have touched more human lives than any other man in history since the days of the New Testament. Had it not been for Aldergate, the world might have never heard of John Wesley. Wesley himself could never forget the place. The house in Aldergate Street was the spot where he was changed forever. He could never forget that night.

When he was born in 1703, he entered a world vastly different from the 21st century. If you can imagine a world with no electricity, no railroads or airports, no streetlights, no telephones, no refrigeration or frozen foods, no cars, no free libraries, no aspirin or Coco-Cola–you would see the world of John Wesley. Welfare was unknown. Those in poverty often found themselves incarcerated in filthy prisons for their debts. Schools were very rare and existed for the affluent.

In the heart of secular London on Aldergate Street is a monument in the shape of a scroll, engraved with the testimony of John Wesley.

The conditions of the day for common people were deplorable. *Christian History Magazine* provides for us a vivid description:

"Personal health and cleanliness were deplorable. The plague, smallpox and countless diseases we call minor today had no cures. Most dwellings had no running water, had chamber pots only for elimination, and had no soap, as it was not yet in common use. Infant mortality was extremely high, and a person's life expectancy was in the forties. Clothing was expensive, so many of the cities' poor wore rages that were like their bedding, full of lice."[1]

John Wesley was born June 28, 1703–the fifteenth child of Samuel and Susanna. Not all the children survived. Charles was born in 1707. Charles and John were always devout friends and supporters. When John Wesley was five years old, the family lived in the village of Epworth, where his father was rector of the local church. One night the rectory caught fire and after most of the family had gotten out, they discovered that little John was not in their number. He was still in the burning house. The staircase was blazing, blocking his exit. He got a chair to the window, climbed up on it and called for help. A man was lifted up by others and managed to pull John from the burning fire just in time.

Susanna prayed, thanking God for his safety, and referred to him as a "brand plucked from the burning." She told John that God had saved him for a "purpose." John never forgot the experience.

The rectory was rebuilt and the family resumed their lives in the ministry at Epworth. The boy was ten years old when he was sent to London to Charterhouse School. Later he attended Oxford University to prepare for the ministry.

At Oxford, John and Charles joined with fellow students to form a "holy club." This group met often for prayer and Bible Study, visited the prison and sought holiness through good deeds to the poor. Among their number was George Whitefield, an innkeeper's son from Gloucester. Whitefield later became one of the most noted evangelists in history and profoundly affected the American Colonies.

John had been brought up in a Christian home but had not had an experience with God. He had heard the Bible taught from infancy but still was lost. He had attended the University of Oxford and participated in the "holy club" but was still lost. He had been ordained for the ministry–lost. He served as assistant to his father at the Epworth church–lost. John had confused salvation with religious life and deeds. It had not yet occurred to him that more was needed.

In 1735, Samuel, John's father died. Samuel had been a faithful servant of God. For thirty-nine years, he had pastured the church at Epworth. On his deathbed, Samuel called for John. He knew that something was missing in John's life. Samuel said to him, "Seek for the witness of the Spirit, son." John promised that he would. John knew about works and doctrine but the living Spirit of God was not in him. His father knew it.

That same year John and Charles Wesley went with General Oglethorpe to Georgia. Oglethorpe was a distinguished soldier and had agreed to lead in the organization of the English colony at Savannah. Being

John Wesley went to Georgia to serve as a missionary to the Indians. However, the Indians were reluctant to convert and the colonist resisted the rigid disciplinary type of ministry.

acquainted with the Wesleys, he invited John and Charles to accompany him. Charles would serve as his secretary and John would be chaplain to the colonists. John also hoped to serve as a missionary to the Indians. Landing at the outpost of Savannah, John was met by a Moravian minister named Spangleberry. Spangleberry questioned him, "Man are you saved?" John tried to avoid the question but the Moravian was persistent. Eventually John faked a positive answer but knew in his heart that he was not spiritually secure. John had written in his journal that he was going to Georgia to convert the Indians but also in the "hope of saving my own soul."

The ministry in Georgia was a failure. The Indians were reluctant to convert and the colonist resisted the rigid disciplinary type of ministry. After two years, in February 1738 John fled Savannah under cover of darkness to return to England. The witness of the Moravians still lingered in John's mind.

On the journey to the colony, the ship had gotten into a violent storm at sea. John was terrified of losing his life, but a group of Moravian believers sang, prayed and exhibited complete calm. That impressed him. Then Spangleberry's challenge cut a cord deep in his heart upon arrival. During John's brief stay in Georgia, he could not understand the consistent joy of the Moravian believers in their daily lives.

On the voyage back to England he pondered it all, writing in his journal, "I went to America to convert the Indians, but, oh, who shall convert me?"

The man who had been brought up at the feet of Susanna Wesley in a minister's home, an ordained minister himself, a missionary, still was lost without the Living Spirit of God in his soul.

After arriving back in England, Wesley was befriended by another Moravian, Peter Bohler. Bohler urged Wesley toward a personal faith in Christ. That personal faith came on May 24, 1738, at a house on Aldergate Street. At a prayer meeting John Wesley experienced something he had never experienced before. He encountered Christ as a living person.

Peter Bohler

In the heart of secular London on Aldergate Street is a monument in the shape of a scroll, engraved with the testimony of John Wesley.

"In the evening I went very unwillingly to a society in Aldergate Street, where on was reading Luther's preface to the Epistle to the Romans. About a quarter before nine, while he was describing the change which God works in the heart through faith in Christ, I felt my heart strangely warmed, I felt I did trust in Christ, Christ ALONE, for salvation; and an assurance was given me that he had taken away my sins, even mine, and saved me from the law of sin and death."

Now it all came together. Now he understood what his father, Samuel, was trying to tell him on his deathbed. Now the words of Spangleberry at Savannah made sense. John had been brought up in a Christian home–LOST. He had studied for the ministry–LOST. He had gone to the mission field to win the heathen–LOST. After all of this, at a prayer meeting on Aldergate Street, that which was LOST had been FOUND. The young man had passed from death to life.

Wesley wanted to reform the Church of England. He soon found every door in the Church of England locked in his face. He returned to his home church at Epworth where his father had pastured for thirty-nine years and where he, himself, had been assistant. The minister refused to invite John to preach. That Sunday morning, the minister preached against "religious enthusiasm." As the members left the building after the service, one of Wesley's helpers announced that John Wesley would preach at 6 pm on his father's tombstone, just outside the building. At six that evening the largest crowd Epworth had ever seen appeared in the churchyard to hear John Wesley preach.

In the months that followed Wesley went to the open air. He preached in town squares, mines, streets and fields. People told lies and spread rumors. Some said he was a bootlegger of gin. Others spread rumors that he had committed suicide and that the real Wesley had died.

John Wesley was a little man with a powerful voice. He weighed 128 pounds and was just five feet, three inches tall.

It has been stated that Wesley saved England from a "French type" revolution. The English people were on the verge of such a revolution. They were downtrodden and abused. Wesley brought God to the common people and then they did not need a revolution.

Soon after he died, there were forty million followers. Many of the ice box parish churches stood almost empty but through towns and villages of Britain in little chapels, here and there, Gospel fires were burning. He preached 40,000 sermons, wrote 400 books, traveled on a horse a quarter million miles for God. The world had become his parish.

Wesley preached in town squares, mines, streets and fields.

When John Wesley lay dying on his bed in London, those around him heard him say, "Best of All– God is with us." God had been with him in distant places, in hostile situations. God had been with him when all the worlds rejected him. God had been with him over rugged seas and over hundreds of thousands of miles on horseback. Now at the end of the journey, Wesley felt and knew the presence of Jesus.

I walked away from Aldergate Street that day with joy. I remembered MY Aldergate years ago in Georgia.

Do you remember YOURS?

1 *Christian History Magazine*,
Volume 2, Number 1, p. 7, 1983.

Village of Llanfihangel in Wales

Journey to Bala!

*The true story of
Mary Jones from Wales*

She was only 15 years old when she started the journey. To a little girl walking alone, that twenty-five mile journey from Llanfihangel to Bala was foreboding. The year was 1799 and the west coast of Wales was much more desolate than today. The mountains were rugged and uncultivated. Mary, leaving the cottage, must have felt her heart beating fast as she thought of the long trip to Bala. Mary knew that she had to go. Her mind was made up. She would not waver. She had waited so long for this day. The end of the journey would justify all. The treasure she would find there would dwarf every fear of the journey.

Mary's mother was perplexed. She felt that the road was too rough and dangerous for her daughter to go alone. Mary answered, "I shall not be alone. Jesus says, 'I am with you always.' He will be walking with me." Mary's father, Jacob, replied, "Mary is right. God will take care of her. We have to let her go or we may be found fighting against God."

That morning Mary had awakened early. After washing and combing her hair, she dressed for the journey. This was the most important day of her life. Her mother and father were waiting for her arrival at the table. After the breakfast was over, her parents knelt with her in prayer, asking God to keep her safe and protect her on the way to Bala. After kissing them goodbye, Mary walked from the cottage barefooted to begin her journey. In her bag she had her shoes but would use them sparingly on the journey to avoid wearing them out.

For assurance Mary quoted verses she had committed to memory. "I will lift up mine eyes unto the hills, from whence cometh my help." "My help cometh from the Lord, which made heaven and earth."

Mary Jones was 15 when she started the journey.

"He that keepeth thee will not slumber nor sleep." "The sun shall not smite thee by day, nor the moon by night. The Lord shall preserve thee from all evil."

Soon she would be able to read these words from her own Bible. That Bible was twenty-five miles away–in Bala. For six long years Mary had prayed for a Bible. Those years of working and saving for this day now seemed like a dream. She was on her way. Mary thought, "I am going for my Bible! I am really, really on my way to get my Bible! I can hardly believe it."

The first part of the journey was familiar ground. Soon, however, the scene became strange. The road seemed empty and the countryside lonely with little signs of habitation. In her book Mary Carter described the scene.

"Here and there she saw a lonely farmhouse, or caught sight of a shepherd and his dog high up on the slopes of Cader Idris; but for the rest she was the only moving figure in the whole vast empty landscape. The track grew wilder as she climbed the shoulder of the mountain, and Mary had to scramble over boulders, sometimes making long detours where the path was blocked by a fall of rock. She stuck to it gamely, and at last was rewarded. She came to the brow of a hill and looked down on the valley beneath. It had been a stiff climb and, as she stood gazing round her, she seemed utterly alone on the bare shoulder of the mountain."[1]

The little girl now saw a world that looked very big. The trail down the mountain was easier. Now Mary began to see more farms and people.

As Mary was trudging along, her mind wandered back to her first encounter with the Bible. Her parents were Godly Christians and often rehearsed what verses they could remember from the mission meetings.

As Mary made her way along the trail, she thought about those meetings. She remembered stumbling with her mother through the darkness with a lantern, making their way to those meetings when she was only eight years old. Mary was always a delight in those meetings.

She listened and sang as intently as any adult present. Coming home, she would rehearse the Scripture to her ill father word by word. She told her mother that she would love to have a Bible. Then she added with a sigh, "But I couldn't read it, could I?"

At that time there were no schools anywhere near the village of Llanfihangel where the Jones family lived. Also there were few Bibles available in Wales in the Welsh language. Jacob, her father, was a weaver and very poor, as most of the people were who lived in the villages of Wales.

It was a day of survival with no frills. Books were rare and expensive and only for those with means and education. Mary often prayed that she could one day

For assurance Mary quoted verses she had committed to memory. "I will lift up mine eyes unto the hills, from whence cometh my help."

learn to read so that she could read the Bible for herself.

Mary thought with delight of the day her father returned from Abergynolwyn, a nearby village where he had gone to sell his goods. He brought home the news that Mary might soon be able to read and write. There was going to be a school opened at Abergynolwyn. Mary remembered her joy. She remembered rising early in those days to do her chores before embarking on the two-mile walk to school.

All of that was six years past. She could now read and she was on her way to Bala for her Bible. Passing through the villages, she would ask those she met, "How far is Bala?" With Bala still being miles away, they would reply, "Oh you are going to Bala–that is very far. You must hurry to be there before dark."

Increasing her pace, Mary held to her bag tightly. She must not lose her money for the Bible. She had worked so long and so hard to save that much money. Her mind wandered back over the six years of work and prayers involved in accumulating that money.

She thought of the afternoon when she returned from school and her father presented her with a moneybox. Mary was delighted. Inside were two halfpennies, one from him and one from her mother. He explained, "We wanted to be the first to put something in." Over the six years Mary did special work for anyone to add to the money in her special box. She helped neighbors, did washing and ironing and special chores to save. Little by little, coin by coin, the funds grew.

Now trudging along the country trail, Mary thought of the day when she had

saved enough to buy a Bible. She was told by a minister that a minister in Bala by the name of Rev. Thomas Charles had copies. There were few copies of the Bible in all of Wales but Rev. Charles, he told her, had some.

At last Mary reached her destination. Her pastor back in Llanfihangel had directed her to go to the Methodist preacher's residence. He was sure he would help her. A kind woman whom she met on the road directed her to the preacher's home. When the minister opened the door, he was surprised

"I love the Bible. I have loved it ever since I was a little girl and heard it read at meetings when I went with my mother and father."

to find his late visitor standing there. After Mary explained, he invited her in and listened intently to her story. He said, "Mary, tomorrow we will go to see Rev. Charles. He lives just across the street. He rises early. I know he will help you in any way possible." The kind minister and his wife prepared food and lodging for her that night.

Mary was shown to her room. That night she thanked God for her safe journey before stretching her tired limbs out to rest. She thought, "God has kept me safe and tomorrow I am going to get my Bible." With that beautiful thought Mary fell into a deep, restful sleep.

It seemed only a moment had passed when Mary heard Pastor Edwards knock on her door. It was morning and breakfast was ready. At breakfast Rev. Edwards said, "Mary, Mr. Charles' light is on in his house across the way. I think we can go over to see him."

They crossed the street where Thomas Charles lived and knocked on his door. Mary's heart was in her throat. The kind man immediately invited them inside with the comment, "This is an early visit. I hope all is well." The Methodist minister explained that Mary had come a long way to see him.

Rev. Charles looked down at the little girl, noting her poor clothing and roughened hands. He thought that she had probably come to request work or financial help. He asked Mary why she wanted to see him. Now that she was actually face to face with him, her confidence faded.

The Methodist minister endeavoring to help said, "Mr. Charles, this young girl, Mary Jones, has walked all the way from Llanfihangel, near Abergynolwyn, to ask if you have a Bible you can spare her." Mary Carter furnishes a vivid description of this event in her work:

"A Bible!" said Mr. Charles, interested at once. "Tell me, child, can you read?" "Oh yes, sir," answered Mary. "I have not long left Abergynolwyn School." "Then you learnt under Mr. Ellis," said Mr. Charles. "Yes, sir," Mary replied, "and Mr. Lewis Williams." "That is very good," said Mr. Charles. "I am interested in Abergynolwyn. And you come from Llanfihangel. Do you live with your parents?" "Yes, sir," answered Mary, feeling much more at ease now that she was speaking of her own home and the places that Mr. Charles also knew. "My father and mother are weavers."

"Now tell me," said Mr. Charles, "how is it that you have made this long journey in order to buy a Bible? Do you know anything of the Scriptures?" "Yes, sir," answered Mary, her eyes sparkling. "I love the Bible. I have loved it ever since I was a little girl and heard it read at meetings when I went with my mother and father.

Then the school opened, when I was ten, and I learned to read; and a Sunday School started too, and I went. But I needed a Bible more than ever then, and a kind friend, Mrs. Evans, promised that when I learned to read I could go and study her Bible at the farm. So I went, every Saturday, to study my Sunday-school lesson. The farm is up the mountain, two miles away."

"And you walked two miles every Saturday to study the Scriptures," said Mr. Charles. [2]

Mary went on to tell that she had learned the parables and much of the Sermon on the Mount. As Mary spoke, her face glowed with deep earnest conviction and sincerity. Thomas Charles was deeply touched. He had rarely seen such a deep devotion in anyone like this of any age.

Mary Carter continued her description. "And you have come all the way from Llanfihangel to buy a Bible," said Mr. Charles. "Yes, if you please sir," Mary answered quietly. "I have the money here in this purse."

"But, if your parents are weavers, and not, I suppose, very rich, how could you have got so much money as a Bible now cost?" asked Mr. Charles.

"I worked and saved for six years," Mary answered. "I minded children, I did mending for neighbors. I picked sticks. I kept chickens. Oh I did everything I could to save enough."

Rev. Thomas Charles stared at Mary in awe. All of his words left him. After a few moments of silence he said to the Methodist minister, "Oh, friend Edwards! To see this young girl, so brave, so intelligent, so consistent a Christian, coming all this long twenty-five miles to me for a Bible, and I have none to spare for her, not one. And there is no hope of getting one. The Society has refused to print any more Bibles for Wales."

The Methodist minister exclaimed, "Don't you have even one for this girl?" Charles replied, "No not a single one. I have three Bibles in that bookcase, but they are all promised out."

Mary could not believe her ears. God would not let this happen. In a flash all the years of working, all the prayers, all the dreams were all crumbling. The long road to Bala–the long road home–with empty hands–and no Bible. She burst into tears and wept uncontrollably. She buried her face in her hands so as to hide her emotion, but floods of tears flowed through her fingers and dropped to the floor.

The two ministers sat in silence, not knowing what to say. Then Rev. Charles stood to his feet. Placing his hand on Mary's head he said, "Mary you will have your Bible. I cannot send you away empty, no matter who else goes without a Bible." With those words spoken, he walked to his bookcase, opened the door and retrieved one of the precious three Bibles.

Taking Mary's hand, he opened her fingers and placed the Bible in her hands. Mary looked up at Rev. Charles, her eyes still brimming with tears and asked, "Is it really for me?" "Yes, this Bible is for you," he replied. "May God bless you as you read it." He then turned to his Methodist friend and said, "This illustrates the need for Bibles in Wales. I will never rest until I get Bibles into this country."

After a meal with the Methodist minister and his wife, Mary departed Bala with her Bible safely stored in her bag. With her own Bible, she was on her way home. In the years that followed, Mary read the Bible

Mary Jones died in 1866.

"Mr. Charles," he said, "your appeal has moved us all very much. The story of that young girl is truly heart-rending and hers is the story of the world. You speak of your hope of forming a society for printing and distributing Bibles in Wales; but I say, if for Wales, why not for the world?"

Out of that meeting, on December 7, 1802, was born the British and Foreign Bible Society. Returning to Wales, Rev. Thomas Charles made his way again to Mary's cottage. After greetings had been exchanged, he told Mary and her parents that her story had touched the people in London and through the new Society would ultimately touch the world–and it did. The British and Foreign Bible Society led the way for the National Bible Society of Scotland (1826), the American Bible Society (1816), the Bible Society of the Netherlands (1814) and others.

Mary Jones taught in Sunday School for many years. She died in 1866 at the age of 82. Mary Jones never lost her zeal and love for the Bible. That burning fire and quest for truth embedded in the heart of a little girl from Wales–lit a fire whose flames have lit the world.

With a new generation born every day and with a population of 6 billion souls on planet earth, we must redouble our efforts to distribute the Word of God to the perishing multitudes who have never heard.

through. She realized for the first time that the Bible was a continuous story. Daily she read to her parents.

Thomas Charles could not get the scene out of his mind. Once visiting Mary's village, he paid a call to her home. He asked Mary to pray for him as he was going to London to plead for more Bibles. Charles did go to London. There at a meeting of the Religious Tract Society he told the story of Mary Jones. He finished his speech and sat down. The members had listened with intense interest. Then a Rev. Joseph Hughes rose from his chair.

1 *Mary Jones and Her Bible*, revised and rewritten by Mary Carter, The British & Foreign Bible Society, London, 1949.

2 *Mary Jones and Her Bible*, 72 - 73 revised and rewritten by Mary Carter, The British & Foreign Bible Society, London, 1949.

The Ultimate... Journey!

The bus station below the hill seemed almost as if it would burst with it pressing transient population. The hordes of people pushing between large vehicles and *en route* to destinations were totally unaware of my presence or my notice of them from the hill above.

Long ago other crowds hurried past this very point below this hill. They too were *en route* with hardly a passing glance up the hill. That day long ago the presence of those up above on the hill generated little more than a curious glimpse.

I had followed the steps of greatness throughout America and Europe. I had surveyed the footsteps of Brainerd, Judson, Livingstone, Meyer, Spurgeon and others whose footsteps of faith and courage inspired me. I had walked in footprints of blood and climbed through dungeons. I had surveyed

the darkness and felt the iron chains. I had visited their graves.

The trail of the faithful and martyrs merged from a thousand directions until the many paths blended into one road–*Calvary Road*. Those footsteps had led here to this hill above the bus station. More realistically the thousands of footprints had not merged into this road to Calvary but *out* from it. These were the footprints of those who had followed the steps of Christ and who had gone throughout the earth. *They* had noticed the hill and had been *changed forever* for their notice.

I retraced the ultimate steps from the cave at Bethlehem to the well at Samaria–to the Sea of Galilee–to Gethsemane and at last to this hill. What happened here?

This hill represented the center of eternity, the central point from which all time pivots. The man dying up on the hill was called Jesus.

In the Old Testament God revealed Himself by **Numerous Names**. A name tells all about a person–his family, background, his roots. But what ONE NAME could describe God's roots when He is eternal? What ONE NAME could tell FINITE MAN about an INFINITE GOD?

In Exodus Moses at the burning bush asked God **what His name was**. God replied, **"I am the LORD"** (Jehovah–the "Existing One").
"I have always been."

The first words of Scripture begin with "In the beginning, GOD...." The word *God* there is "Elohim," meaning "Greatness and Glory–Omnipotence. God was saying, "I am all powerful."

Abraham was told to take Isaac, his only son, to the mountain and sacrifice him. He was to slay Isaac with a knife and make him a sacrifice to God. Before the knife came down into the heart of Isaac, however, God stopped him. God had arranged for a ram to be caught in the thicket. That ram would be the sacrifice instead of Isaac. God revealed Himself that day to Abram as **"Jehovah-Jireh,"** meaning "The Lord will provide." God was saying to Abraham, "I am the God who will provide."

There are **12 names of God in the Old Testament**, all describing one who cannot be described in mere words.

These were those who had followed the steps of Christ and who had gone throughout the earth. They had noticed the hill and had been changed forever for their notice.

Ask Adam, "Who is God–what is His name?" He would reply, "God is ELOHIM–THE ALL POWERFUL ONE."

Ask Abraham, "Who is God–what is His name?" He would reply, "God is Jehovah–jireh"–THE ALL PROVIDING ONE."

Ask Moses, "Who is God–what is His name?" He would reply, "He is "Jehovah–THE EVER EXISTING ONE."

Throughout 4000 years of human history, there were not enough names to describe One such as God whom the Heaven of Heavens could not contain. Finite man could never put One so great in a name or a **word**.

THEN CAME THE DAWNING OF THE NEW TESTAMENT and the Rivers and streams of the continents finally found their way to the ONE GREAT OCEAN–(JESUS). The stars and planets locked in their orbit around the great sun. All the ships made the Harbor. The Scribe at last combined all the volumes containing the wisdom of the ages into one. He closed his book and laid down his pen. The cover read JESUS. The mysteries of all ages were UNVEILED by a birth at **Bethlehem**.

The Wise men and star gazers for 4000 years had searched the heavens and then they found the STAR they had been looking for. They came to Herod and said, "WE have seen His star in the east."

All the names of God were gathered up and poured into One–**THE NAME**

JESUS. The Name of Jesus and the Person of the Father are welded together by ISAIAH WHO SAID: "For unto us a child is born, unto us a son is given: and the government shall be upon his shoulder: and his name shall be called Wonderful, Counselor, The mighty God, THE EVERLASTING FATHER, The Prince of Peace." (Isaiah 9:6, KJV)

The Apostle Paul explained it this way: "For in him dwelleth all the fullness of the Godhead bodily." (Colossians 2:9, KJV)

Paul said we have reached the end of our search—In Jesus BODILY IS ALL OF GOD WE SHALL EVER NEED TO KNOW.

Calvary

That body, then, dying up on the hill represented all of God that there was. This hill had been the starting point of all the footprints I had retraced. The spring had enlarged into a stream. The stream had widened into a river. The river had made its way to the great ocean, touching every shore and flooding every land.

Millions had been caught in the wake of its flood and were washed and redeemed.

That redemption was reflected in the words of Cowper:

> *"God moves in a mysterious way*
> *His wonders to perform;*
> *He plants His footsteps in the sea*
> *And rides upon the storm."*

The echoes of Calvary resounded into a mighty, universal chorus of the redeemed.

The dungeon glowed with light, as so profoundly described by Wesley:

> *"Long my imprisoned spirit lay*
> *Fast bound in sin*
> *I woke - the dungeon flamed with light!*
> *My chains fell off, my heart was free,*
> *I rose, went forth, and followed Thee."*

The guilty souls sighed relief:

> *"There is a fountain filled with blood*
> *Drawn from Immanuel's veins,*
> *And sinners plunged beneath that flood*
> *Lose all their guilty stains."*

The slave trader who showed no mercy and knew no grace turned in his whip for a cross and wrote:

> *"Amazing grace! how sweet the sound*
> *That saved a wretch like me!*
> *I once was lost but now am found,*
> *Was blind but now I see!"*

The atheist threw down his infidel writings and picked up the Book of Hope. The forsaken embraced a "Love that would not let him go."

The blind reveled in visions of light. As Bunyan's pilgrims, the great throng marched upward toward the Celestial City of Light, taking with them millions on the…

Ultimate Incredible Journey to Heaven!